# THE SELF-COMPASSION COMPANION

30 WAYS IN 30 DAYS

## DR. PAIGE RAWSON

Copyright © 2025 by Dr. Paige Rawson

All rights reserved.

No part of this book may be reproduced in any form or by any electronic or mechanical means, including information storage and retrieval systems, without written permission from the author, except for the use of brief quotations in a book review.

Tehom Center Publishing is a 501(c)3 nonprofit publishing feminist and queer authors, with a commitment to elevate BIPOC writers. Its face and voice is Rev. Dr. Angela Yarber.

Paperback ISBN: 978-1-966655-04-6

Ebook ISBN: 978-1-966655-05-3

## CONTENTS

| | |
|---|---:|
| *Introduction* | ix |
| 1. Acceptance, Authenticity, Affirmation | 1 |
| 2. The Broken and/as the Beautiful | 5 |
| 3. Body Boldness | 9 |
| 4. The 3 Cs: Consciousness, Curiosity, & Compassion | 13 |
| 5. Connection & Creativity | 21 |
| 6. Courage and/in Coming Out | 25 |
| 7. Comparison, Competition, & Contentment | 29 |
| 8. Doubt, Depression, & Derailing Damaging Self-Talk | 33 |
| 9. Empathy toward Empowerment | 37 |
| 10. Fear, Faith, & Freedom | 41 |
| 11. Forgiveness | 45 |
| 12. Grace for the Grief | 51 |
| 13. Hurt, Healing, & Home | 55 |
| 14. Inspiration & Infinitude | 59 |
| 15. JO(urne)Y | 63 |
| 16. Kin-dness | 69 |
| 17. Liberation in Love | 73 |
| 18. Mindfulness in Movement | 77 |
| 19. Nurture through Nonjudgment and Nonabandonment | 83 |
| 20. Openness | 87 |
| 21. Purpose & Poise | 91 |
| 22. The Power of Presence | 95 |
| 23. Queer(y)ing | 99 |
| 24. Rest for Renewal | 103 |

25. Self-Care as Self-Preservation and Self-
    Determination                                    107
26. Sympathy toward Solidarity                       111
27. Wholeheartedness                                 115
28. Xenophobia                                       119
29. Yes And, Hell, No!                               125
30. Zen                                              129

*Epilogue*                                           133
*Acknowledgements*                                   135
*Appendix*                                           137
*Bibliography*                                       163
*National Helpline Numbers*                          167

*For my clients, my partner, and my little self.
You inspired me to write this book and live its truths.*

*Perhaps
we should love ourselves
so fiercely,
that when others see us
they know
how it should be done.*
*— Rudy Francisco*

# INTRODUCTION

This tiny book is a labor of love and a love letter from me to you. As a self-compassion coach and a self-love practitioner, I am committed to compassion as a lifestyle because it saved my life. I wrote this book for the same reason I coach clients toward self-compassion: my life was transformed by it, and so I have devoted my life to educating, equipping, and empowering others with the tools to transition from self-loathing to self-love. In my mid-twenties, after years of self-destructive behavior and self-sabotaging beliefs (including that my worth was bound up in external validation) I was hospitalized for a month and almost died. Until this life-altering event, I had no idea my deprecating thoughts and dysregulated emotions were serving to sustain the sickness in my body. While my diagnoses and the care offered me during my hospitalization made a decisive difference, what ultimately healed me were the healthy habits I formed in the months and years after I was discharged. I developed rituals and routines to aid me in identifying and dissolving the walls I had built to protect myself;

walls that prevented me from living, giving, and receiving love. Though they vary in size and strength, we all have walls and the quotes, reflections, and practical applications I offer in this book are a way to work with and walk through those walls. What I share with you in the following pages are parts of my story and the foundation of what has become a thriving self-compassion practice. This book is also my gift to you on your self-love journey, which is why I call it *The Self-Compassion Companion*.

I sincerely believe this book has the potential to transform your life precisely because it contains resources to help you access and activate the single most powerful force for change known to humanity: love. As a species, we evolved certain traits for survival. Fear, self-criticism, and the negativity bias function as evolutionary adaptive responses. Even as they serve to protect and preserve us, however, they inhibit our individual and collective progress. Research reveals fear and self-criticism can prevent us from developing a healthy self-concept and meaningful connections, pursuing new goals and opportunities, and living a happy and fulfilled life. I believe the most effective way to transcend fear and self-criticism—and, therefore, thrive as a species—is through love and, specifically, compassion and compassion directed toward ourselves enables us to authentically love others. (When we know we are safe, seen, and supported, we can settle into our skin and extend the same reassurance to others.) While we may not have been raised in a loving, compassionate environment, we can learn how to live a loving and compassionate life, and the single most effective way to cultivate genuine compassion for others is by practicing on ourselves. In my opinion, if we were all to practice self-compassion, we would heal ourselves and our world.

As my partner pointed out, people do not need directions to read a book. As a former pastor and professor, however, there are three things I have been trained to consider as I approach any audience: social location, communication, and expectations. While I may not yet know your name, context or identity, it is important you know mine, so you know the location from which I see, speak, and write; something that should always be considered when we engage (the ideas of) others. It is also imperative that I provide as much information as I can to make this experience as enjoyable and efficacious as possible. I am a queer, neurodivergent, white, former evangelical pastor and professor with a PhD, who has practiced self-compassion for over two decades to heal my relational and religious trauma. As you will notice, these pieces of me influence how I understand and engage the world—at the intersection of self-compassion and social justice, where the former animates my commitment to the latter. Whether or not you can relate to my particular roles or wounds, I believe you will find resonances between your story and mine, since suffering is a universal experience and self-compassion is the central source of all our healing.

Throughout the book, I use the words "love" and "compassion" liberally and interchangeably along with "lovingkindness." I will briefly clarify the distinction here and go into greater depth throughout the book. Love is broadly understood as affection; from the Indo-European root *leubh*, which means "to care for" or "to desire." In distinction, compassion is taken from the Latin word *compati* and means "to suffer with." Love and compassion, then, might be said to differ not by quality but by degree. We might also think of this distinction through the metaphor of the sun, where love is the sun and compassion one of its rays. (The Greek language has eight different words for love, ancient Persian has eighty, and Sanskrit has ninety!) If love is caring or expressing affection toward a particular object, then compassion is caring so much you are willing to *suffer with* the object of your affection. It follows, then, that self-love is caring for ourselves, and self-compassion is caring for ourselves enough to sit in tender care with *our own suffering*. Love gives us the courage to open ourselves to connecting and, therefore, potentially being hurt by another. Compassion renders us truly vulnerable to feeling our own pain and that of others with strength enough to hold space for the hurt without becoming more discouraged, damaged, or deterred by it.

Being human can be challenging. Every new day brings new experiences and for some of us the struggle might be compounded by other social, economic, and psychological factors that affect our mental health as well as our emotional and physical well-being. We encounter other humans, their emotions and ours, inconveniences and emergencies, we have errands and obligations, and so many choices that there are at least five different English terms to describe the overwhelm we experience because of it. Arguably, the most important of all the decisions we make in a day is the very first; that is, how we will approach it. When we choose to engage our day and ourselves with love, compassion, and kindness, rather than fear, criticism, and negativity, we free ourselves to live in the strength of our vulnerability and to comfort ourselves rather than condemn ourselves in the face of discouragement or disappointment. Research has proven the negativity bias is beneficial in the short term to ensure our survival, but in order to thrive in the long term, we require the capacity to identify and absorb positive information, and to validate and love ourselves. It has been said that what we feed grows and what we starve dies, so if self-effacement and negativity are what we feed, they are also what we breed. For the next 30 days of your life, I invite you to instead feed on love and self-compassion. Rather than fueling rejection through self-criticism and fear, use this book as a companion that will lead you in offering yourself loving-kindness and empathy every single day.

In the pages that follow, you will find quotes, reflections, and exercises meant to educate you—teacher's gotta' teach!—and guide you through daily meditations on love. Every entry has a different theme that centers self-compassion and opens with words from someone who learned to love themselves in the face of great obstacles. I offer ruminations which provide information and inspiration on that entry's theme, meant to engage your mind, your heart, and your body and to motivate you to critical thought, mindful self-reflection, and compassionate action. At the end of each entry, there is a contemplative grounding practice, which includes a mantra, meditation, or invitation offering practical application to help you integrate self-compassion into your daily routine. Some entries close with questions for reflection, so keep a notebook close. I realize journaling does not appeal to all, but putting pen to paper has as many mental health benefits as exercise or therapy, including mindfulness, stress and anxiety management, emotional regulation, creative expression and coping

INTRODUCTION

with depression. In addition to a bibliography with relevant self-compassion resources, I have also included a list of national helplines for your convenience.

In closing, you may proceed to read in whatever way feels right for you—cover-to-cover in a few sittings, choosing a page or number at random, one day at a time, or picking a relevant topic in the Table of Contents. (While each subsequent entry builds upon the last, all of them stand alone and can be read in any order.) I believe the most effective way, however, is to open the book when you wake, possibly while enjoying your favorite morning beverage in a quiet and comfortable location (if that is available and accessible). Take ten to twenty minutes to read one entry, complete the exercise, and allow the practice to center you as you move into the day. In this way, you will set the tone for your day and can return and reflect at any moment, remembering and relaxing into self-compassion whatever you encounter.

There is no limit to what we can do when compassion is the focus of our meditation and becomes our deepest motivation. As you live, as you read, let love lead.

— Paige

# 1

# ACCEPTANCE, AUTHENTICITY, AFFIRMATION

"If you can't love yourself, how in the hell are you gonna' love somebody else?"

— RUPAUL

ACCEPTANCE IS THE FIRST STEP OF PERSONAL transformation and a hallmark of radical self-love. RuPaul's words are an iteration of a truth conveyed in many great spiritual traditions around the world and throughout time: we must love ourselves to love others. Unfortunately, many of us have been taught to understand self-love to be synonymous with selfishness, particularly those of us who are Black, Indigenous, and People of Color (BIPOC), were socialized to be women, and/or raised Christian. The conflation of self-love with selfishness is, in my opinion, a form of gaslighting. While "gaslighting" has become colloquial, it bears defining since it is so common and effective that it often operates undetected. Gaslighting is a form of psychological manipulation where the abuser seeks to sow seeds of self-doubt in their victim. When a trusted authority associates self-love with selfishness, the individual under their influence subconsciously equates any attention or action directed toward themselves or their self-care with pride and egoism. For example, women have historically been encouraged to spend their time and energy in the service of their children and husband; any effort made to tend to themselves was, and often still is, deemed self-serving and unproductive. The same self-sacrifice, however, is not as celebrated in men, who are often excused and even encouraged to put themselves before others. While a woman/mother is expected to sublimate her dreams and desires in service of family, committee, and community, a man/father is praised when he does so because he is "exceeding expectations." The travesty is, however, in this sort of imbalanced relational and emotional economy, even the most advantaged among us suffer.

As a society, all of us are suffocated by social agreements that are enforced rather than intuited. Dominant culture ensures our compliance through various means, including social norms, demanding our bodies do certain things and act in certain ways. As a result, it requires a tremendous amount of energy and courage to remain true to oneself and, thereby, subvert the system. RuPaul George is exemplary in this regard, maintaining his integrity and refusing to conform to the societal expectations of a (Black) man. Though RuPaul has faced fierce critique, even withing the drag community, by staying true to himself and deploying drag as a medium for defying heteronormativity, he has not only created a safe space within and for himself but has inspired gender non-conforming queer folks in and beyond the drag scene in their disruption of the binary gender system. One might say RuPaul's self-love was so big it made room for others to love themselves; his self-acceptance, authenticity, and the affirmation of his queer identity have inspired others to live into their own.

The root of "inspiration" is the Latin word *inspirare*, which means "breathe into." Another way to understand RuPaul's words and the truth of radical self-love and acceptance, that loving myself inspires me to love others, is through the directive given by flight attendants when cabin pressure is lost. Even as I employ this metaphor, I acknowledge it may not be or feel relatable, since flying is a privilege only 20% of the world can afford, it may also seem to oversimplify self-love or to be an extreme example. I believe, however, that our planetary predicament is an extreme emergency because compassion is as important to our species as oxygen is to our planet, yet so many of us do not practice because we've been conditioned to reject or protect ourselves and prioritize or villainize others. The directive given by flight attendants is that each person put on their oxygen mask before assisting another, since we are of no help depleted or dead. If oxygen in this metaphor is love, then, it is impossible to genuinely love another if you cannot love yourself, and loving yourself means you accept (love from) yourself. For those of us gaslit into self-deprecation, conditioned to put others first, and who are now responsible for other lives both in and outside our homes, we desperately need breathe in this truth: loving yourself is the path to and power behind loving others, you cannot love them if you do not love yourself.

DR. PAIGE RAWSON

Today, take a deep breath of the above truth and let it fill you like oxygen. Focus upon radical self-acceptance in exchange for self-rejection. Take a moment to do the following: Place your hand on your heart and repeat the following phrases to yourself as many times as you need today: *I love you, [insert your name], I appreciate and affirm your unique way of being human, and I accept you just as you are.* If you feel led, take ten minutes today to write yourself a love letter. It need not be long, but it is time you acknowledge and articulate all the things you adore about yourself. Allow the radical acceptance of your authentic self to inspire the affirmation of your unique identity.

## 2

# THE BROKEN AND/AS THE BEAUTIFUL

"Kintsugi [is] not just a method of repair but also a philosophy. It's the belief that the breaks, cracks and repairs become a valuable and esteemed part of the history of an object, rather than something to be hidden. That, in fact, the piece is more beautiful for having been broken."

— KATHLEEN TESSARO

I GREW UP IN THE UNITED STATES AND, WHILE I WAS taught to respect my elders, everything in my cultural context told me that growing old and frail was something to be dreaded, even feared, because when you are old, you are no longer useful or beautiful. After I graduated college, I moved to Southeast Asia and was exposed to an entirely different perspective on aging and the elderly. The aunties and uncles, who were the same age as my grandparents and great grandparents, were honored and revered; they were also active and very happy. Their stories were not disregarded nor were their bodies discarded upon retirement. Likewise, their wrinkles were worn with pride and their wisdom was shared with joy. Elders did not appear obsessed with youth or remaining young, nor were they seen as disposable or a drain on resources; quite the opposite, they were viewed as resources and treasures to appreciate and even to venerate.

In Asia, this respect for what is aged or weathered translates to inanimate objects too. In America—the number one producer of garbage, with each American generating 4.5 pounds or 2 kilograms every single day—we typically toss out old and "broken" articles or stick them in a recycling bin (the contents of which may or may not get recycled). In Japan, to the contrary, there is a practice of turning the treatment of what one of us in the North America might consider trash into a treasured art form. Japan also happens to be one of the top ten countries producing the least amount of waste per capita. So, not only do the Japanese create little refuse, but they refuse to discard a thing simply because it is aged or cracked, appreciating and accentuating its brokenness as beauty. The art form devoted to the preservation and repair of broken objects is *kintsugi* (金継ぎ, "golden joinery"), also known as *kintsukuroi* (金繕い, "golden repair"). In this method, the artist repairs broken pottery by mending the areas of breakage with urushi lacquer, a natural resin from the urushi tree, that is mixed with powdered gold, silver, or platinum—a process that often renders the item even stronger than before it was broken. While kintsugi is most famously displayed in the restoring of broken pottery, any object can be repaired in this way. This art form becomes a poignant symbol for embracing, emphasizing, and celebrating imperfections rather than concealing them. Instead of denying, dreading, or discarding, kintsugi can help us to dignify (what is) aging.

Reflecting on kintsugi in this way can help shift our perspective toward what feels broken in us and can even help us reframe the aging process. What if, against American cultural values, we were to see our failures and setbacks, wrinkles and cracks, as an important part of what constitutes us as lovely and worthy of love? What if the failure, hurt, and disappointment we have experienced are not the ugliest or worst parts of us, but our most redeeming qualities? What if you and I honored the very things that have led us to feel broken and reprehensible and came to understand them instead to be where our true strength and beauty lie? Self-compassion, in this way, is like kintsugi in that it transforms our broken into beautiful.

---

Today, practice kintsugi on yourself. The focus here is not fixing but feeling. Identify an area of your life that feels broken or a way you feel disrespected and/or disposable. Find a picture from that season or see it in your mind's eye and extend yourself compassion. Let your affirmation be: *I honor and embrace what feels broken in me as beautiful. I choose to bring what has caused shame into the light of my love. I will take pride and find power in those parts I have previously perceived as unacceptable. I will self-celebrate rather than self-deprecate. All parts of me deserve to be loved, so I will love every part of me—the broken and/as the beautiful.*

## 3

## BODY BOLDNESS

"and I said to my body. softly. 'i want to be your friend.' it took a long breath. and replied, 'i have been waiting my whole life for this'."

— NAYYIRAH WAHEED

AROUND 2012, AMID THE ME TOO AND BLACK LIVES Matter movements, another Black women-led movement emerged that also rejected violence against BIPOC (and) women, as well as Western standards of beauty, through the celebration of Blackness, brownness, thickness, and fatness. The Body Positivity Movement, like its counterparts, had roots in the 1960's, alongside the Civil Rights, Black Power, Gay Liberation, and Women's Rights movements. Inaugurated by fat, queer, Black women who demanded rights and respect in a society denying them both, the movement's rebirth reflects the social moment and has gained traction among people of all races and ethnicities, plus-size and otherwise. Like many countercultural BIPOC-led movements, there has been legitimate concern over the Body Positivity Movement's co-opting by white people. Therefore, I write this entry in honor of its roots, acknowledging the entwinement of racist, sexist, heteropatriarchal and colonialist ideologies in relation to ideas on the body and beauty, and elevating Black women's voices and their impact, even on me as a gender queer white person.

Johnnie Tillmon, leader of the original movement, once said, "I'm a woman. I'm a Black woman. I'm a poor woman. I'm a fat woman. I'm a middle-aged woman. In this country, if you're any one of those things you count less as a human being." Her words bring into sharp relief the intersectionality of oppressions and how white supremacy culture makes it exponentially harder for BIPOC, poor, fat, old, and disabled women to not only live, but love themselves. Black women like Tillmon, Roxane Gay, Sonya Renee Taylor, and Simone Mariposa are champions of body positivity, who embody radical self-love as a path to liberation. To love your body is bold when dominant culture identifies white thin cis-gender heterosexual bodies as beautiful and, therefore, ideal. The great irony is that the norm is not, in fact, normative—only 5% of the world is white, thin, cis and hetero. To add insult to injury, social media now equips us with tools to make us appear "perfect" when no one is. The unrealistic standards of beauty imposed upon us by the white male minority with institutional authority inhibit us all from living authentically and loving ourselves completely.

As a temporarily able-bodied white queer person who prioritizes listening to, learning from, and uplifting the voices of People of Color, especially queer Black women, and has been positively influenced by the Body Positivity Movement, I want to share my deep appreciation for it. Watching, reading, and witnessing the bold proclamations of self-love and self-determination made by queer and straight Black women, both in and beyond the Body Positivity Movement, has played an integral role in me radically loving and enthusiastically living into my queer body—a body that never has conformed to the norms inflicted upon it and halle-fucking-lujah it never will! (Thank you, Althea Spencer Miller and Sonya Renee Taylor!) Witnessing what these women have overcome to embrace and celebrate their identity and their bodies, inspired me to the same. I understand the Body Positivity Movement, like BLM and Me Too, to represent a shift in consciousness for individual and collective transformation with something to teach us all. It is time we honor the voices long silenced and suppressed, the peoples who have survived centuries of oppression, for they are the ones with something profound to teach us, especially about radical self-love. Identity unequivocally influences how we interpret and are interpreted and our bodiliness inflects and informs our experience of the world. We may be limited by our individual bodies in the ways we see, interpret, and move in the world, but when we embrace our bodies boldly in self-compassion there is no limit to what we can do together.

---

Today, consider the messages you have received about bodies, beauty, and what makes a body beautiful. Acknowledge the lies meant to disempower you, preserve power dynamics, and/or perpetuate systems of oppression. You and your body are beautiful. Rather than rejecting your body, befriend it and revel in your body and the ways you move and occupy space. Write your body and its parts a letter of love and affirmation to replace the damaging messages. Finally, spend time today moving your body in a way that makes you feel bold and beautiful!

# 4

# THE 3 CS: CONSCIOUSNESS, CURIOSITY, & COMPASSION

"In cultivating loving-kindness, we train first to be honest, loving, and compassionate toward ourselves. Rather than nurturing self-denigration, we begin to cultivate a clear-seeing kindness…Without loving-kindness for ourselves it is difficult, if not impossible, to genuinely feel it for others."

— PEMA CHÖDRÖN

IN LEARNING TO LOVE THE PARTS OF ME I DO NOT LIKE, I created a practice to aid in shifting from judgment and self-criticism to kindness and self-compassion. I call this method "The 3 Cs." Today's entry is longer because I briefly explain the Inner Critic and Core Self, give an example of a message from my Inner Critic, walk through the 3 Cs—engaging the Core Self to respond to the Critic's voice—and, finally, offer a prompt to apply them in your self-compassion practice.

When we feel we have failed or fucked up, one of the hardest things to do is remain present and mindful, since we are hardwired to seek pleasure to avoid pain or, alternatively, to spiral into self-hate. What often compounds our distress is that we are not only dealing with the issue at hand, but other people's opinions as well as the voice in our head that may be leading us to believe we are to blame. While we cannot control other people or their impressions, we can work with what is happening inside us. The Inner Critic is the voice on the committee in our head and the part of us who identifies flaws and faults to prevent us from failure and rejection and, at times, finds us culpable; quite often this voice is the result of socialization and/or trauma. While the Inner Critic is working to protect us from vulnerability to embarrassment or attack, the Core Self responds to perceived threats through courage and compassion. Like the names for God in different cultures, there are various terms used to represent the Core Self; though the vocabulary may differ, we are describing the same reality. The Core Self is the pure conscious energy of our authentic openhearted state of being and, as such, is the seat of compassion, curiosity, calm, creativity, clarity, confidence, courage, and connectedness. These eight characteristics of the Core Self that let us know when we are operating from an authentic openhearted state rather than out of our defenses or inhibitory emotions (anxiety, guilt, and shame). These attributes are always already available to us in our Core Self, grounding and reminding us of the truth of who we are, especially when the Inner Critic gets going. Here is an example of the voice of my Inner Critic:

*Who cares what you have to say, Paige. There are many other more intelligent, articulate, and attractive people conveying their insights in a more relevant and riveting way than you ever could. Sit down, shut up, and save yourself the disappointment.*

Ouch! The Inner Critic is the expert on criticism and comparison and could do it round-the-clock. Rather than giving the Inner Critic unlimited airtime, acknowledge it, and apply the 3 Cs.

The first C is *Consciousness*. Becoming conscious of the Inner Critic is the initial step. We cannot affect change until we see clearly what we are facing. When we can become aware of this voice, we can work with it. The first time I recognized the voice of the Inner Critic is the result of introjection (or the unconscious adoption of external judgments) rather than my Core Self everything changed because I also realized:

1. My Core Self and the Inner Critic are not the same,
2. I always have a choice how I respond to the Inner Critic,
3. The power to do so comes from the Core Self, and
4. The Inner Critic and its messages only have power over me if I listen and believe them; recognizing this is the epitome of consciousness.

The second C is *Curiosity*. The way I understand and explain this step to clients is: if the Inner Critic is looking for blind spots—trying to identify your weaknesses to protect you—your Core Self responds by seeking understanding through curiosity and clarity rather than the Inner Critic's modalities (criticism, comparison, or condemnation). Knowing how each voice operates makes it easier to distinguish between them. In this step, we get to know ourselves by exploring what is coming up for us. Am I getting defensive or experiencing anxiety, guilt or shame? Once we become conscious of the Inner Critic, we non-aggressively and nonjudgmentally inquire into the origin of these thoughts and the purpose they serve, which can move us to identify and feel the underlying emotions triggered. Amicability is important here because the more we approach ourselves antagonistically, the louder and more chaotic the Inner Critic becomes, which can trigger a shouting match in the brain's boardroom, exacerbating anxiety and leading us to storm out, shut down, or spiral in shame and suffering.

I have been engaging my Inner Critic and the above message for years, so I have a lot of practice. My goal is no longer to chase my Inner Critic away, I now seek to befriend it. Here is an example of how I respond when my Inner Critic attacks: "I see you and I hear you. You seem anxious and are working hard to protect me by leaning into some old messages. What are you feeling underneath the harsh words you are speaking? Have you felt this before? When? How does it feel to connect with that younger version of me? What else is coming up in this? Is there something specific that frightens you? If so, could you walk me through it and help me understand what you need and what would help right now?" Talking to yourself in this way might feel like learning a new language to some of us, it could seem silly to others, or maybe it excites you. Regardless, I encourage you to experiment and will give you the opportunity to do so below.

The third C is *Compassion*. While the focus here is on self-compassion, it is present throughout the process. This final step, however, is when the Core Self really shines because it loves to love, and it really loves to love *you*. Give yourself the same grace, gentleness, and understanding you would someone very special to you. The application of compassion is integral because as we explore and expose the most tender parts of ourselves, and allow ourselves to feel anger, sadness, fear, or disappointment, we often crave a tender touch. It feels amazing when another human can offer this affection, which is why the support of a therapist, life coach, spiritual teacher or healer, and, of course, our loved ones is invaluable. The most radical realization we come to in this work, however, is that you and I are the source of love and, therefore, our own healing. In fact, this is often the greatest benefit of having skilled, intuitive professionals on our team—they aid us in understanding our capacity to love and to heal ourselves.

I honor and appreciate that some of us are neurodiverse and/or struggle with mental and emotional disabilities. Self-love, however, is not something accessible only to the upper class or able-bodied. In my experience, the most qualified and effective self-love practitioners have been lower or middle class, neuroatypical, and/or disabled. In fact, I believe the people who love themselves the most are the ones who have had to fight the hardest to do so; present company included. Just as we are all capable of self-compassion, we all struggle with our Inner Critic. Even those of us who have been at this work for years struggle at times with insecurity and cognitive distortions that show up in the form of imposter syndrome, performance anxiety, self-doubt, personalization, and comparison. I find that when I get defensive about inner work, it is one of my parts trying to protect me from further suffering. What I now realize is that the more I push the pain away, the more suffering I create for myself and others. Therefore, when this happens, I offer reassurance from my Core Self. Letting myself know it is safe to proceed, I offer compassion toward all my tender hurting and healing parts; in so doing, I enact the courage I need to face and embrace myself and whatever obstacles and adventures lie ahead.

---

Today, set aside time to identify the voice of your Inner Critic and to engage your Core Self, working your way lovingly through the 3 C's. First, bring into *Consciousness* the voice of your Inner Critic by reflecting on a negative message like the one I shared above. Next, get *Curious* about the message and its origins as well as what you need in this delicate space. (You may refer to my inquiries above.) Finally, tap into radical *Compassion* by offering yourself the lovingkindness and nurturing only you can. Remember, you know yourself better than anyone, which means you have exactly what it takes to meet your own needs. Let that resonate and release you to relax into love as you find the words you need to hear to replace those self-critical messages. Since this practice is one way to rewire neural pathways, there will likely be resistance and discomfort, and your Inner Critic may get activated and agitated. I find the louder the voice of my

Inner Critic, the more (often) my Core Self needs to speak up, so in engaging today's exercise find a place you feel safe to vocalize these courageous and compassionate messages, maybe even out loud. Feel free to write these messages down and return to them. It may feel awkward and uncomfortable, but I assure you it works!

5

## CONNECTION & CREATIVITY

"The worst enemy to creativity is self-doubt."

— SYLVIA PLATH

IN HONOR OF THE MULTIFARIOUS WAYS CONNECTION breeds creativity, today's entry is a collection of quotes from various creatives in addition to my voice. It concludes with an ideational exercise meant to inspire you especially in seemingly uninspired seasons, which are a part of life. As much as we may wish to be perpetually productive, we, like all of life, have cycles. We expand and we contract; this is true organically, energetically and artistically. We have all experienced despondency and despair, days where we lack the motivation to connect or create. If, as Sylvia Plath suggested, self-doubt is creativity's worst enemy, then, self-love is creativity's closest companion. Doubt, detachment, and dissociation inhibit our creative process. Experiencing disconnection from ourselves, our ecosystem, and other sentient beings can block us energetically, and prevent us from accessing abundance and feeling our way into flow. During these times, rather than forcing ourselves to connect or create, research reveals that loosening our grip on a particular problem and allowing ourselves to release expectations for specific outcomes allows new options to emerge; herein lies the energy for ingenuity, transformation, revitalization, and revolution. As you read the following quotes, relax into the wisdom of others and open yourself to what emerges in the encounter. May these words resonate, educate, and invigorate:

> "Life is pure adventure, and the sooner we realize that the quicker we will be able to treat life as art: to bring all our energies to each encounter, to remain flexible enough to notice and admit when what we expected to happen did not happen. We need to remember that we are created creative and can invent new scenarios as frequently as they are needed."
>
> — MAYA ANGELOU

> "Creativity is our most powerful tool to shape the world we want to live in."
>
> — ISRA HIRSI

> "Creativity comes from trust. Trust your instincts."
>
> — RITA MAE BROWN

"Be wild; that is how to clear the river. The river does not flow polluted, we manage that. The river does not dry up, we block it. If we want to allow it its freedom, we have to allow our ideational lives to be let loose, to stream, letting anything come, initially censoring nothing. That is creative life. It is made up of divine paradox. To create one must be willing to be stone stupid, to sit upon a throne on top of a jackass and spill rubies from one's mouth. Then the river will flow, then we can stand in the stream of it raining down."

— CLARISSA PINKOLA ESTÉS

"Make visible what, without you, might perhaps never have been seen."

— OPRAH WINFREY

---

Today, direct your attention to your heart center. To the best of your ability, tune into the energy you emit and honor the creative life force within you. From this generative place, do one or both of these exercises for the next 5-10 minutes: Reflect on the quote that most moves you, write about what about it inspires you (to create), and one thing you would like to create in the next year of your life. If that exercise doesn't speak to you and you're in the mood to doodle, take out a blank piece of paper or use the following page of the book and get a pack of crayons, markers, or color pencils. Create as many 1-inch circles as you can (they don't have to be symmetrical) and sketch different shapes and recognizable objects inside each circle. Feel free to get as playful as possible! Once you've filled every circle, reflect on the following questions: Which circles do you like in particular? Do notice any patterns as you appreciate your artistry? Do any of the circles connect or did you draw connections between them? Take a moment to see to see if there is any way to connect some of the similar or seemingly dissimilar circles. Sometimes creativity comes through uncommon and unexpected connections, keep a look out for those today.

## 6

# COURAGE AND/IN COMING OUT

"Love makes your soul crawl out from its hiding place."

— ZORA NEALE HURSTON

ALL OF US HAVE "THOSE DAYS," WHEN WE FEEL LIKE crawling into our favorite hiding place and avoiding the world. Most days, we do not have the option, some days, however, that is just what we need. Those of us who know the pain of being an outsider, particularly those of us dehumanized for our difference, have learned how to survive in inhospitable environments. Some of us were led to believe we are unworthy of love, others have been too hurt to trust, and many know the burn of both. It is imperative, therefore, that we learn to love ourselves by understanding what we need and advocating for it; allowing ourselves time and space to shelter in safety and cultivate the courage (and support) to step out of hiding and speak our truth; only we know the right time and we have the right to choose (for) ourselves.

Several entries touch upon making time for self-nurture in solitude. Today, the focus is self-nurturing as stepping out of the closet. The metaphor of coming out can apply to the various ways any of us courageously comes out of hiding and stands in our truth. In my opinion, "coming out" is not just "a gay thing." Internal Family Systems (IFS) labels the hidden part(s) of ourselves "The Exile." The Exile is our vulnerable inner child, who, due to unhealed trauma, is in hiding. The Exile, then, represents what we have repressed and suppressed to protect ourselves and preserve attachments. According to IFS, the way to liberate, or unburden, the Exile is for the (adult) Self to meet the Exile in their trauma and re-parent them, offering a compassionate safe space to release and bring all parts back into harmony. Healing, then, involves recognizing, accepting, and embracing the traumatized, fearful, and rejected part of ourselves. The Exile must come out but can only do so through the compassion of the True, or Core, Self.

There is tremendous risk in rendering ourselves vulnerable by making visible what was previously kept secret, particularly the qualities we are conditioned to consider deviant or undesirable. Those of us whose difference has historically defined us as unacceptable have been more vulnerable and, therefore, susceptible to violence—which is what compelled us to conformity and complicity in the first place and why so many of us remain in hiding. American culture does not celebrate difference as much as it supports and sustains those upholding the status quo. To be non-normative is as shameful as it is dangerous and not all of us have the privilege of passing, making life even more difficult for BIPOC, trans, and disabled people. The threat of physical or emotional harm is inherently fear-inducing, so sharing the shameful parts of ourselves must be predicated on love, which is why it is vital that when we make the courageous decision to come out of isolation, we nurture ourselves and/in relationships where we are understood, validated, and accepted. I personally did not begin coming out as queer until I was in my mid-twenties, and it was only because I got so sick my secret almost killed me and was finally with people and in a place where I was safe enough to share the truth of my whole self. Love, and specifically self-compassion, gifts us the courage to come out.

---

Today, I invite you to consider the closet as metaphor in your own life. Close your eyes, take three deep breaths, and connect with the fearful, ashamed part of you. See your Exile in the proverbial closet. What does this tender part of you feel here and what does it need to feel, hear, and know to feel safe enough to come out? Place your hand on your heart and connect with your Core Self. Keep your hand on your heart and imagine there is a glowing sphere of light emanating from your chest and radiating with love. As you access the love inside you, with your mind's eye, see your exiled inner child coming out of the closet and into the light. Feel the light of your love shine on your sweet little face, inside and all around you. Take three more deep cleansing breaths and sit in this space of safety and self-compassion. Coming out is a process and is not a one-time event. It takes time. As you continue to practice this sort of compassion, you will gain the courage to come out of other closets of silence, secrecy, and shame. There is no need to force yourself out, be gentle. You will open the door when you are ready. Loving yourself involves even and especially the parts you've previously found unattractive and unworthy. Continue to connect with each part and to hold yourself in the same sort of tender care you would a newborn baby, a wounded animal, or a disheartened friend. The more we love what we hide or consider shameful, the more we want to love and share those parts of us.

7

# COMPARISON, COMPETITION, & CONTENTMENT

"People are starving for love, not knowing their heart is a magical kitchen. Open your heart. Open your magical kitchen and refuse to walk around the world begging for love. In your heart is all the love you need. Your heart can create any amount of love, not just for yourself, but for the whole world."

— DON MIGUEL RUIZ

IN AMERICA, WE ARE CONDITIONED TO EVALUATE ourselves through the lens of capitalism, we own our body as a means of production by which we make money to survive. As a result, our worth has become inextricably linked to our productivity and external validation. Even the language we use to express the significance of a human life is that of commodification: the English word employed to represent how we feel about ourselves—self-*esteem*—derives from the Latin word *aesti-*

*mare* and signifies the estimation or appraisal of one's value or worth. Because we have been programmed to assess human value according to ability and usefulness, any characteristic limiting our capacity to produce is interpreted as a deficiency (à la ableism). As much progress as we have made intellectually and technologically, it is time we evolve in this area too, no longer linking the significance of a life to its ability (to generate capital). Like maturation in any other area, to evolve, we must become conscious of how we have been unconsciously sustaining this system, which feeds off our feelings of worthlessness demanding we produce to be worthy, even of love.

In *The Mastery of Love*, Don Miguel Ruiz offers an allegory on love, encouraging his reader to imagine they have a magical kitchen with an endless supply of any food they desire. Ruiz, then, presents the reader with a conflict. Imagine you forget you have access to this kitchen, and someone comes with a pizza, offering you all the pizza you want with one contingency: you must do whatever they ask. When you are unaware you have access to all the food you want and more, you might become convinced you need this other person and what they offer to survive, abandoning yourself and acquiescing to their will just to have your needs met.

The Magical Kitchen symbolizes what we all have inside, an infinitely renewable resource many of us rarely recognize as such: love. According to Ruiz, if we were to understand the presence and power of love within us, we would not settle for anything less than love in every area of our life. Unfortunately, in a society and economy that favors individualism to collectivism and conceptualizes the human being as commodity, we are conditioned to perceive our world and relationships through commodification rather than compassion, where we compare and compete more often than connect and collaborate. As a result of our social conditioning, many of us move through life with an implicit fear of scarcity and intense feelings of unworthiness, leading to greed and the hoarding of our possessions, on the one hand, or restricting and punishing ourselves for our desires, on the other. This faulty framework results in further alienation from our implicit power and genuine presence and leads to greater isolation from community and real connection, not to mention it breeds craving and prevents us from being content with who we are right where we are. When we come to truly understand and accept that love is an inside job, external validation and the acquisition of material wealth may be important and even enjoyable, but they no longer control or consume us because we know to our core that they can never nourish us.

---

Today, indulge in your Magical Kitchen. Abundance is not somewhere outside you; it has always been right here within you. Take a few minutes, now, to reflect upon your life as if it were a movie and answer the following questions in your journal: What are the important scenes and people in the plot of your life? When have you loved and felt loved? Has there been an event or a person who led you to believe you are alone and unlovable? Imagine yourself responding to this event or person from the abundant place of love and compassion rather than scarcity or unworthiness. How does it feel and how does this change the situation and your response to it? Take these final moments to pleasure in the love that fills you and flows from you.

## 8

## DOUBT, DEPRESSION, & DERAILING DAMAGING SELF-TALK

"Doubt is a pain too lonely to know that faith is his twin brother."

— KHALIL GIBRAN

My childhood was characterized by an endless amount of energy and an insatiable curiosity. Unsettled by my effervescence, some adults in my religious community cast my questions as doubt and succeeded in stifling some of the most glorious parts of me, at least for a little while. I will never know the alternative had I been given the chance to explore those imaginative inquiries, to commend rather than condemn my curiosity, or had I been told that Jesus, like the Buddha and Socrates, asked exponentially more questions than he answered. Instead, I suffered for decades under the thumb of a damning inner critic, led to believe my doubt was diabolical and a sign I could not trust my deceitful heart—just *one* of the ways I was gaslit by the Gospel. My doubt was turned against me as I was led to believe it was just another quality that disqualified me as a person of faith. And so, during my childhood, adolescence, and early adulthood I was haunted by sabotaging self-judgment, alienation with/in my spiritual community, and a depression that ultimately led to my hospitalization.

In my mid-twenties, however, as I was exposed to more information, experiences, and global perspectives (and with the maturation of my prefrontal cortex), I started to view myself and the world through a vastly different lens. I stumbled across an article on Mother Teresa of Calcutta, a woman whose life of faith had always inspired me. In this expose were excerpts of letters she wrote to a reverend wherein she shared candidly about her crisis of faith. This altruistic human, eventually canonized for having devoted her life to living out her faith in service of the impoverished and infirmed of India, struggled with doubt, despair, and disappointment because she could not see or even feel God. Let me repeat: Mother Teresa, a woman of faith, who lived her life in service of God and the disenfranchised, doubted (the existence of) God!

When I read her honest and heartfelt confessions, something in me shifted. For years, I was led to believe doubt occluded and precluded faith. In learning the truth about Mother Teresa, I was given hope and the revelation that faith and doubt are inextricably linked. While there were several factors that led to my recovery from toxic, exclusivist theology to the more gracious approach (toward myself and the world) of an openhearted and radically inclusive spirituality, the catalyst was that article on Mother Teresa. Knowing her faith was not doubt-free led me to deconstruct the version of faith upon which I had been raised and to open my heart and arms to people of all faiths. It also enabled me to immerse myself fully in my own unique faith journey where faith was not about verifying the existence of a God, but being present to God in myself and others.

I, like so many others, was gaslit by the toxic ideology of the ecclesial institution because I was persuaded to believe that I was untrustworthy, and my doubt was a device of the devil that deterred me from "the truth." Once I allowed myself to doubt what others claimed was truth rather than doubt myself, I came to apprehend the opposite to be true. I realized my doubt was rooted in a deep knowing I could trust more than institutional authorities and external sources of validation. My doubt was an implement and extension of my wisdom, which led me to challenge any system that would have me obey indiscriminately and emboldened me to move through my depression and away from damaging self-talk. Before I could heal, the pendulum swung hard in the other direction, and I went through a period where I doubted everything *but* myself, and especially any voice that disparaged me. Then, gradually, as I continued to grow and reintegrate, I learned what and who I could trust, how to derail self-deprecation, and right when I needed to celebrate myself and others.

---

Today, I'd like you to use my experience to reflect upon and write about the parts of you that have been questioned, critiqued or condemned that led you to self-doubt and damaging self-talk. While you may not be able to relate to my personal experience of doubt, every one of us has encountered it in some iteration. What has your experience led you to believe and doubt about yourself? Are there ways you have negatively labeled yourself or self-deprecating phrases you have used as a result? Please take a moment to connect with the way self-doubt has manifested in your life as an adult. What might this less secure part of you tell you about yourself and what words do you need to hear from yourself in this moment? As you consider how these painful relationships and experiences might have contributed to damaging self-talk, how might you reframe these words or phrases through self-compassion? Now, give yourself permission to redeem the qualities you were led to believe were weaknesses that could instead be celebrated as strengths. We have spent too many years allowing others to define us. Today, and every day after, let us commit to redefining and rejoicing in ourselves! As Rachel Rodgers so eloquently put it: "We are the saviors we are waiting for!"

# 9

# EMPATHY TOWARD EMPOWERMENT

"To simply think about the people, as the dominators do, without any self-giving in that thought, to fail to think with the people, is a sure way to cease being revolutionary leaders. Because love is an act of courage, not of fear, love is a commitment to others."

— PAULO FREIRE

IN 1968, PAULO FREIRE PUBLISHED ONE OF THE MOST influential texts in critical pedagogy, *Pedagogy of the Oppressed*. Freire, an educator and philosopher, critiques the banking model of education, wherein students are programmed to receive and regurgitate information, in favor of a problem-solving approach, which empowers students to participate in the pedagogical process. It is not enough to think *about* those we teach, lead, and serve, Freire invites us to think *with* them. The difference between *thinking about* and *thinking with* is found in the distinction between knowing as an intellectual activity versus knowing as an embodied experience rooted in empathy; the former is a claim to consideration while the latter is characterized by the capacity to understand someone's lived experience. Empathy derives from the Greek word for suffering (*pathos*) and, like compassion, signifies being with another *in* (*em-*) their suffering. One way to understand *thinking with* is in how "we the people" vote. Constituents often vote for a member of their political party who looks like them—which, of course, was not really an option for BIPOC, woman, or LGBTQ+ people until the mid-twentieth century. Even now, though white men make up only 30% of the US population, they take up 85-90% of US government. Since people are statistically more likely to trust someone who resembles them—assuming a leader's experience and, therefore interests (i.e., policy) will most closely reflect their own—70% of the population has had to trust leaders to empathize with them and protect their rights, when those leaders cannot directly relate to their experience. It is evident in the legislation and diplomacy of the twenty-first century that many of our politicians' politics are not governed by empathy.

Freire's pedagogy challenges us to consider how we might think *with* someone who bears no resemblance to us, as well as how we might address systemic inequities and revitalize our educational and political institutions. In individualistic cultures like America and Great Britain, great attention is paid to personal success and how one might improve their appearance, reputation, and social standing. Collectivistic cultures, like Freire's Brazilian context, place more emphasis on the good of the whole. In a collectivist frame, out of respect for the interconnected nature of all life, individual success and security are regarded in relation to the whole. Thriving or flourishing, then, is not defined by achieving personal wealth or happiness, but is found in a commitment to others, which strengthens the entire community. A leadership paradigm that radically decenters self is the mark of a truly (self)compassionate human and, according to Freire, a revolutionary leader. How might America(ns) grow if we integrated this framework and were led *by* compassion to lead *with* compassion rather than competition and conceit?

Oprah Winfrey once asserted, "Extending yourself in compassion to another human being changes the nature of your relationship…the acknowledgment of one human being to another is what bonds, strengthens, and expands the human connection." Compassion, as empathy, not only transforms the nature of interpersonal connections, it fortifies the network of humanity, enhancing universal consciousness and our ecosystem. We all long to be a part of something bigger than ourselves—a community, a vision, a movement. Unfortunately, when that desire is not directed by self-compassion it leads us to believe that "bigger" is found in growing our reputation, bank accounts, and/or social media following. I can think of nothing bigger or better, worthwhile or honorable, than contributing to the betterment of humanity and our quantum entanglement through the courageous act of compassion, which refuses the isolation of radical individualism and empower us all.

Today, reflect on Freire's words in relation to you and how you live, love, and lead in the world. Even if you don't consider yourself a leader in the traditional sense, you have influence. When have you thought or felt *with* someone else and particularly a person or people who bear no resemblance to you? How might you engage in compassion in this way today? Possibly even consider in what practical way you may involve yourself in a project or new group that has a commitment to compassion through action in the local or global community.

## 10

## FEAR, FAITH, & FREEDOM

"Don't move the way fear makes you move, move the way love makes you move."

— RUMI

HUMANS ARE ANIMALS AND, AS SUCH, WE REACT TO WHAT we perceive as threatening or harmful like every other animal on Earth; our acute stress response is fight, flight, freeze, or fawn. One important feature differentiating us from other sentient beings, however, is our cerebral cortex. The cerebral cortex contains the parietal, occipital, frontal, and temporal lobes, is the outermost part of our brain, and is responsible for higher cognition—including reasoning, thought, and decision making, as well as language, memory, learning, emotion, intelligence, and personality. The incredible extra gray matter we have equips us with the unique ability to process external threats and respond rather than react. While this is not true for those of us who have had damage to our cerebral cortex, it is the case for around 95% of humans.

I have often wondered whether understanding this critical difference might help us make better decisions for ourselves and our planet. Would this knowledge aid us in interpersonal communication and cross-cultural correspondence? Could it benefit us in creating more ethical relationships, businesses, and governments or even prevent conflicts from road rage to war? I now believe having this knowledge is not enough, since it is not new information—we have known about the cerebral cortex since the late nineteenth century. Possessing information alone is inadequate for true growth. Yes, "knowledge is power" (thank you, Sir Francis Bacon), but knowledge is insignificant and unremarkable if not coupled with compassion, and power does not lead to liberation unless imbued with love. American and Western European history has given us enough evidence to know this to be true.

Long before I had studied history from a global perspective, I thought the antithesis of love was hate; I am now convinced it is fear and that hateful acts stem from fear. I am also acutely aware that some people may claim to be acting out of faith in God but could unconsciously be motivated by fear stemming from inaccurate information and insufficient experience. I think this is evident when we look at the so-called ministry of someone like Fred Phelps or the way homophobia, Islamophobia, and gynophobia still have a foothold in America. There is a biblical text that reads, "There's no fear in love, but perfect love casts out fear." In this same text, the writer asserts that "God is love." It bears noting that this notion shows up in many other faith traditions, including Islam and Judaism. There is a somewhat universal belief that fear is antithetical to the divine nature and to faith. If faith is trust in God and God is love, and if love is liberative, then, faith flourishes in love and true people of faith/God would never insult, exploit, enslave, or exterminate others because those are acts of fear not of love. Gaining information can often help us face our fears, but overcoming fear is found in understanding its source and befriending the fear and the source of the fear that holds us captive. In so doing, we are liberated, as Rumi asserts, to move with/in love.

Rumi was a Sufi mystic who sought to emphasize the unifying power of love and used his poetry to build bridges across cultures and religions. The great poet believed "our task is not to seek for love, but merely to seek and find all barriers within yourself that you have built against it." Through self-compassion we can understand the source of our fear, extend ourselves empathy for the walls we have erected for protection, and begin to build boundaries or even bridges rather than barricades. As we do so, we can gain the faith to operate freely as ourselves in the world. Instead of being consumed by fear and reacting adversely to perceived threats, we can encounter difficult people, systems, and experiences and exercise choice by responding to ourselves and others with compassion. "For to be free," according to Nelson Mandela, "is not merely to cast off one's chains, but to live in a way that respects and enhances the freedom of others."

Today, acknowledge and appreciate both the fear and the divine in you. Notice your fear and your reaction to it. Where does it manifest in your body? Choose to respond from a tender heart of compassion and wrap your arms around yourself in a loving embrace. As compassion frees us from fear, we gain the profound ability to feel and express compassion toward others—the epitome of incarnating the divine.

## 11

## FORGIVENESS

"Love is that condition in the healing spirit so profound that it allows us to forgive."

— DR. MAYA ANGELOU

THIS ENTRY HAS BEEN THE MOST DIFFICULT TO WRITE because forgiveness is arguably one of the most complex processes we navigate as humans, particularly during or in the aftermath of abuse. Dr. Maya Angelou once proclaimed: "Love recognizes no barriers. It jumps hurdles, leaps fences, penetrates walls to arrive at its destination full of hope." In a way only she could, Dr. Angelou paints a picture of love as effervescent resilient body, bounding over any obstacle to ensure its intentions. While love might just be the only force powerful enough to break down the barriers of fear, hatred, and injustice, and end all forms of abuse, and it may even move the most fragile heart to forgive, love never demands it. Forgiveness is an important part of healing and an act of self-compassion, but even Desmond Tutu, who wrote multiple award-winning books on forgiveness, understands forgiveness as a process that cannot be expected of someone suffering ongoing abuse. In today's ruminations, I honor the historic and continual suffering of indigenous peoples and invite you toward compassionate contemplation on the relevance of forgiveness for you through this lens. This entry is about forgiveness, but even more, it is about making room for our own pain and the pain of others at the same time.

For nearly fifty years, Archbishop Desmond Tutu struggled alongside Mandela to end apartheid; advocating for Mandela's liberation and, eventually, his presidency. Mandela and Tutu, through the Truth and Reconciliation Committee, led South Africa toward reform, reparation, and reconciliation—this was only possible, however, through the partnership of Black and white South Africans (Afrikaners), who, together, ended apartheid and established a democratic South Africa. Many have drawn a parallel between South Africa and Palestine-Israel, including Mandela, who famously stated, "We know too well that our freedom is incomplete without the freedom of the Palestinians." Reconciliation in South Africa hinged on Afrikaners honoring the humanity of Black South Africans as equals, taking responsibility for systemic racism and an inequitable political system, and supporting a new inclusive government. Repair and reform are impossible when the offending party refuses to take responsibility and defends oppression as just. In the same vein, forgiveness, while important, is not the key to healing nor is it even recommended for anyone being actively victimized by an abuser who repudiates accountability.

In *The Book of Forgiving*, Tutu identifies four features

of forgiveness, which do not apply to victims of ongoing abuse. Tutu encouraged Black South Africans to move toward forgiveness only *after* apartheid ended. Research suggests forgiveness has many health benefits but is not necessary for healing—either for survivors of trauma or those currently enduring abuse. So, while Tutu encouraged Black South Africans to forgive Afrikaners, indigenous peoples need not forgive colonial settlers, just as the victims of domestic abuse need not forgive their abusers. Self-compassion is knowing what you need and trusting yourself to feel and heal in your own time, which is my final caveat before turning to Tutu's words. Forgiveness is a byproduct of love, but should never be coerced, it must be organic to be authentic and ensure a survivor does not continue to suffer but has ample space to heal. Now, Archbishop Tutu's insights on forgiveness (with some of my ruminations):

*Forgiving does not mean forgetting.* Forgiveness is "remembering and not using your right to hit back. It's a second chance for a new beginning. And the remembering part is particularly important…if you don't want to repeat what happened." According to Tutu, forgiveness involves recognition of the conditions in which abuse and injustice emerge(d); a process that also entails the conscientization of victim and perpetrator, which would prevent either party from reenacting the same offense and unjust dynamic in the future. Unless oppressed peoples become conscious enough of the system of their oppression to dismantle it, in the words of Paulo Freire, "instead of striving for liberation, [the oppressed] tend…to become oppressors." That bears repeating. Unless those who have been oppressed fully comprehend the circumstances that led to their oppression and work to circumvent them, if and/or when they gain power, they are statistically more likely to oppress others in the same way they were oppressed. Leading to another aspect of forgiveness...

*Forgiveness means revoking the right to retaliation.* Tutu writes, "Forgiveness does not mean condoning what has been done. Forgiving means abandoning your right to pay back the perpetrator in his own coin." In oppressive dynamics, there is an imbalance of power, which implicitly disallows the victim to retaliate in the perpetrator's coin; a victim may subvert, resist, or rebel against their oppressor but oppression is directly linked to the egregious abuse of power. Once the victim is emancipated and has access to the means to get revenge, Tutu points out that forgiveness entails the revocation of such a right. Healing, however, looks quite different for survivors than victims actively struggling for survival, self-determination, and emancipation. The revocation of retaliation is a right most often enjoyed by one whose abuser is in the rearview, since liberation from oppression requires action.

*Forgiving requires facing reality if there is to be true reconciliation.* Forgiveness and reconciliation, Tutu writes, "are not about pretending things are other than they are...True reconciliation exposes the awfulness, the abuse, the hurt, the truth. It could even sometimes make things worse. It is a risky undertaking but, in the end, it is worthwhile, because in the end only an honest confrontation with reality can bring real healing." For Tutu, forgiveness and reconciliation are connected by the thread of compassion, enabling us "to recognize the unique pressures and singular stories of the people on the other side of our conflicts." While reconciliation is contingent on two parties, forgiveness is a choice we make for and by ourselves.

*Forgiveness is for you and them, but mainly you.* According to Tutu, "Forgiveness is the only way to heal ourselves and to be free from the past. Without forgiveness, we remain tethered to the person who harmed us…bound to the chains of bitterness." Forgiveness can set us free from the past, but not from ongoing violence and abuse. Forgiveness is powered by love, but so is liberation because love levels walls, it frees us—even from being forced to forgive. Dr. Angelou spoke about love in terms of forgiveness because she was set free by love to forgive her past abusers, who were no longer in her life. She understood love as a condition specific to the healing spirit, which empowers the wounded to determine who they are beyond their wound and to forgive because no longer bound to their wounder. Love is the resilience it requires to endure, the recognition of responsibility that facilitates reconciliation, and the strength to say, "no more."

---

Today, reflect upon forgiveness as a self-compassion practice rather than a mandate for healing. Forgiveness is a choice and a process, so check in with yourself and honor your experience. The most compassionate question we can ask is: what do you need? Ask yourself. As you pursue healing, you can trust yourself to know when, or if, it's time. Is there anyone you want to forgive? Is it possible the person you need to forgive most is yourself? It is important we take responsibility for our actions, but we cannot take the onus fully when there are always multiple factors at play. It may also be that you are currently in an abusive relationship and today might just be the day you take the important self-compassionate steps of acknowledgement and asking for help. (Please see the list of helplines in the Appendix.) Take time to consider how you might be blaming yourself for events and circumstances that were not and are not your fault. Breathe through this exercise; just like learning to love yourself, forgiving yourself is not easy. As these instances and emotions surface, place your hand on your heart and repeat the following phrase: *I forgive you, [insert name]. I see you. I love you. I release you. It is not your/my fault.*

## 12

## GRACE FOR THE GRIEF

"To be loving is to be open to grief, to be touched by sorrow, even sorrow that is unending. The way we grieve is informed by whether we know love…Our mourning, our letting ourselves grieve over the loss of loved ones is an expression of our commitment, a form of communication and communion."

— BELL HOOKS

I AM WELL-ACQUAINTED WITH GRIEF AND HAVE COACHED every one of my clients through some form of grief: a lost childhood, the death of a loved one, the end of a romantic relationship, the love they never received from a parent or guardian, being raised in a culture or religion that rejected their identity or individuality, the list goes on and on. Grief comes in all shapes and sizes, ebbs and flows, is non-linear and, at times, entirely incoherent. While grief is inconsistent and unpredictable, three facts about grief are universally true: (1) we all experience grief, (2) we cannot heal without it, and (3) love and grief are significantly correlated.

*First, grief is universal.* Every one of us experiences grief and the pain of loss. Loss is an undeniable part of living, yet we do our best to avoid it through all manner of means and measures. Often due to trauma, some of us attempt to control every aspect of our lives, including our relationships. We strategically police unpredictable variables hoping to circumvent the sorrow that inevitably transpires, railing against things as they are in favor of how we want them to be. While we might believe such efforts protect us, they ultimately require more energy and cause more harm than failing and feeling our feelings in the first place. We will all experience grief, the compassionate thing is to accept grief as an unavoidable part of the human condition.

*Second, all healing requires grief.* Unless we allow ourselves the time and space to feel, we cannot heal. Letting go of anything precious is painful and we will lose precious things. The irony of recovery is it often entails more hurt to heal, which is why close to half of us who begin therapy end treatment within months of our initial session. Those among us who are white and American have become so well-acquainted with comfort and convenience that we expect it—so much so that discomfort, disease, and disappointment often lead us to despondency and depression. A healthy relationship with (the cycle of) life develops from our comfort with and acceptance of loss and death. We know cognitively that everything living must die, but acceptance of and, therefore, healing from the pain of loss is only possible if we compassionately allow ourselves to fully grieve that which we have lost. (For more on grief and its stages, see the groundbreaking work of Elisabeth Kübler-Ross, as well as that of David Kessler and of Claire Bidwell.)

*Third, love and grief are inextricably linked.* In the face of the inevitability of loss and, therefore, suffering and sadness, studies have proven that grief is part of loving and a form of learning with the capacity to build resiliency. Once we accept this, we are better able to cope with the pain of loss. According to Alan Wolfelt, "[L]ove and grief are two sides of the same precious coin. One does not—and cannot—exist without the other. They are the yin and yang of our lives…Grief is predicated on our capacity to give and receive love. Some people choose not to love and so never grieve. If we allow ourselves the grace that comes with love, however, we must allow ourselves the grace that is required to mourn." Grief is not merely an expression of commitment, communion, and communication, but of compassion—toward others and ourselves.

---

Today, reflect on something you've lost. Now, connect with your wisest, most loving self and hold the grieving part of you. Trust your embrace, finding rest in this safe place. While others can offer compassion, no one knows what it feels like to be you better than you. Give yourself permission to be where you are, value and validate your experience, marvel at the wonder you are for what you've endured. When the voices of comparison or disparagement speak up, respond with greater grace for yourself. Remind yourself that your experience is legitimate and to heal, you must feel.

# HURT, HEALING, & HOME

"I imagine one of the reasons people cling to their hates so stubbornly is because they sense, once hate is gone, they will be forced to deal with pain. Not everything that is faced can be changed, but nothing can be changed until it is faced. Perhaps home is not a place but [a] condition."

— JAMES BALDWIN

THE SAYING "HURT PEOPLE HURT PEOPLE" HAS BECOME cliché because of its truth and relevance. Each of us has endured and inflicted pain; though it varies by character and degree, suffering is ubiquitous. While pain can lead us to feel isolated, like grief and fear, it is inevitable and part of the shared human condition. Unfortunately, few of us are taught suffering connects us to others. As a result, instead of opening and inviting people into that vulnerable place, many of us protect ourselves and/or inflict pain on others, so as not to be alone in our hurt.

## DR. PAIGE RAWSON

In my early twenties, I lived in Asia for three years. Though it was not my first time to travel beyond North America, I had never resided outside the US. Within months, I was so riddled with discomfort and fear, my sympathetic nervous system was wrecked. Had I not been immersed in another culture, as a white person, however, I would never have experienced being decentered, living without creature comforts, or having my cultural biases challenged daily, nor would I have benefitted from growing beyond those comforts and biases. While I relocated with the intention of sharing my faith and teaching others, those fragile and formative years gave me the invaluable opportunity to understand and appreciate what other cultures and non-white people had to teach me. I also came to realize my judgment and condemnation of others was inextricably linked to internalized self-hatred. I often say: I went to Asia to save others, but I was the one who got saved.

A young white American woman, who was queer and closeted, I did not realize I had been taught non-Christians were hurting to shield me from seeing how colonialism, white supremacy culture, and Christian theology were poisoning me and our world. In fact, the more I tried to convince Muslims, Buddhists, Hindus, and Humanists they were suffering in their estrangement from God—to prevent them from eternal damnation and join me in the heavenly hereafter—the more I realized I was the one experiencing deep emotional pain. For years, I had been alienated from myself, taught I was innately sinful, and led to believe I should trust male authority figures more than myself. Ironically, it was only by moving away from "home" that I was able to face the farce and find home within myself. Living outside America helped me realize home is not a specific location, not a principality, person, or place. Home is an experience, a condition often cultivated from the inside out, and a healthy home is the primary space for hurt to heal.

I was taught to betray myself for comfort in places they persuaded me to call "home": America, the church, Heaven. Each of these locations, I now see, is a construct, and certainty itself is a sham. We access safe spaces when we trust the home inside us and build relationships with people who have done the same and need not dehumanize or displace others to create "home." Even as hurt people hurt people, healed people heal people, and we do so because, and when, we start with ourselves. As I encounter and engage my pain from the home of my heart, I need not hate myself or you, nor do I feel compelled to change, or convert, either of us. We can just be.

---

Today, take a moment to honor the home that exists within you and, from this safe space, acknowledge an area of hurt in your life (which might have been your own childhood home). Have you experienced any modicum of healing from this hurt? As you access the pain, try to welcome and embrace it as you would a dear friend. I invite you to take a deep breath, paying attention to the rise and fall of your chest and how you are feeling inside your chest (or heart center). Now, if you feel comfortable, repeat the following phrase: *I am love. I am life. I am home.* (Feel free to add any other phrases that feel true and might soothe and reassure you.)

## 14

# INSPIRATION & INFINITUDE

"Traditional Sufi wisdom teaches that we are the creation and manifestation of Infinite Love, and that every event and circumstance of our lives serves to awaken us and remind us that true happiness and security is to be found in the deepest center of ourselves where we are closest to that Infinite Love, where our true needs will be met."

— SHAIKH KABIR HELMINSKI

THERE IS A LOVE POEM IN THE BIBLE THAT MANY OF US recognize, even if the only time we've been to church is to attend a wedding, because it is the most quoted text at nuptials. In this poem, the author asserts that love is patient and kind, not envious, boastful, proud, or rude. The writer also claims that love does not coerce or manipulate, it is not irritable or resentful, love celebrates truth rather than cruelty and, ultimately, that love is infinite. While this is the most popular portion of the text, it is a lesser-known excerpt that inspires today's reflection on love's infinitude. It is this, "When I was a child, I spoke like a child, thought like a child, reasoned like a child; when I became an adult, I put an end to childish ways."

The author of this text links grasping love and its infinitude with maturation, and I would agree—emotional maturity can lead us to embrace and embody love as infinite. I simultaneously believe, however, that children have unfettered access to this revelation, and it is not until they are taught otherwise that they lose sight of love's limitlessness. If, as research reflects, around 80% of American adults are emotionally immature, then, most children in America are raised by emotionally immature parents; what Dr. Lindsey Gibson calls "EIPs." EIPs are children who grew into rigid, defensive, dismissive adults, prone to egoism, anxiety, and resentments. Having themselves been coerced and manipulated by fear—reared in a neo-liberal capitalist society and programmed to prove their worth by competing for attention and accolades—EIPs have little facility for flexibility or nuance. The underdeveloped emotional state of an EIP makes it difficult for them to function in the world, much less access and exercise compassion for themselves or others. Unintelligible through such a nearsighted lens, love often elicits fear for the EIP because intense emotions or the expectation of emotional intimacy can overwhelm and disorganize them, since they may not have received love as children. (Their egocentrism is often the result of having to be self-reliant in childhood.) As a result, somewhere between childhood and adolescence, many of us who are the children of EIPs lost sight of love's boundlessness and, by twenty-five, our (love) light was almost entirely snuffed out.

As we grow, we can unlearn the childhood lessons inhibiting us from living love or allowing ourselves to be loved. One of the gifts of emotional maturity is awakening from the slumber of subconscious self-sabotage into the abundance of our Core Self, whose source is infinite because it is love. When we realize the nature of the Self is love—and can appreciate how our inner child, like all children, lived love before it was conditioned and corrected out of us—we can experience contentment in knowing our emotional needs will be met by the infinitely renewable resource within us all. If we trust this principle, how might it *in-spire* (or breathe new life into) us? What kind of happiness, security, and freedom might we know if we were to accept love's infinitude? What might we believe, become, and create if love were no longer filtered through the lens of neoliberal capitalism? What if we ceased viewing love like territory or time, pieces of a pie to be divided and dispersed, but understood it to be an ever-flowing spring within or an infinite network connecting us all? If love is infinite, then, maybe, like the symbol for infinity, it is inviting us to come full circle again and again as our adult and child selves entwine and integrate, inspired by love's limitlessness.

---

Today, experiment with the idea of love as infinite and your life source. Reflect on a joyful memory of you as a child. If you cannot access one, simply imagine yourself as a child. I invite you to infuse this memory or image with radical compassion for your younger self by sending little you some love in whatever form feels comforting and comfortable for you. One way to practice this throughout the day might be to set three reminders to pause and reconnect with this idea and intention. In closing, I encourage you to take a deep breath and repeat the following phrase: *I am awake. I am infinite. I am love.*

## 15

## JO(URNE)Y

"There is no path to happiness, happiness is the path."

— GAUTAMA BUDDHA

I AM OFTEN ASKED HOW I REMAIN HAPPY IN A WORLD SO full of injustice, pain and conflict, and in a country where the rights of LGBTQ+, BIPOC, immigrants, and women are still threatened, centuries after its inception. My approach is not to ignore these harsh realities or try to escape the truth, but to care for myself amidst these crises and contribute in positive ways whenever and wherever I am able. Happiness, like love, is a choice and an outward expression of the inner experience of joy. Happiness cannot happen when we resist our path or any part of it. I believe the Buddha claimed that happiness was the path because he understood happiness to be an attitude and approach to life. Just like I know there will never be a place or a point in my life where everything is peaceful once and for all—instead I must find the serenity within me—joy is not an objective goal we aspire toward and achieve. Joy is a core emotion, and, like fear, anger, and sadness, it deepens and develops as we nurture it. We cultivate joy on our journey in myriad ways, I do so by staying as present as possible, meditating every day, expressing gratitude, helping others along the road, and connecting with the awe and enthusiasm of my inner child. Today's entry is an homage to your inner child and mine—to their beauty, intelligence, creativity, and playfulness—and to putting them first. If we can learn to walk, dance, or skip, hand-in-hand with our little self, I believe we will come to experience and express true joy in our journey.

When I was younger, I was led to believe a few things about happiness and joy that I have since found to be untrue. The first was to always keep a smile on my face, another was that to be loved I had to be happy, and a third was that to find joy I needed to put others ahead of myself. "J-O-Y," I was told, stood for "Jesus, Others, then, You!" I had no way of knowing these ideas about happiness or this "JOY" hierarchy was harmful nor any way of understanding my relationship to happiness otherwise (not to mention that Jesus himself would have found that taxonomy super cringy); I was just a kid, who trusted the adults around me. I only later realized the whole point of being a kid is to feel all the things, learn how to relate to the world, and to love and enjoy yourself. So many of us were robbed of the innocence of childhood in various ways, we were encouraged to silence or completely shut down the most natural and beautiful parts of ourselves. (For me, it was by elevating others and demoting myself while simultaneously suppressing the ways I wanted to express myself, my gender and sexuality.) When the adults superimposed their structures, supposed to's, and "because I said so's" over our vitality, curiosity, and profound sense of wonder, we lost access to the unfettered joy that characterizes childhood. Though it was covered, it could never be erased. The little you and the little me are still there and, honestly, I believe they hold the key to unlocking our joy in adulthood, but, first, we must be reacquainted.

For many of us, the joyful journey is paved with grief and even anger. This is one of the great paradoxes of life. To heal we must hurt and to access joy, we will know sorrow. I often say our capacity for joy is directly proportionate to our willingness to work with and through our pain and anger; we must feel to heal. I believe this because it has been true for me and so many of my clients and loved ones. There is a fierce resilience and reclamation of joy in historically marginalized communities who have connected with self-compassion for their self-preservation and self-determination. (I also believe this is why Black Joy, Black Girl Joy, Queer Joy, and Black Queer Joy are now a part of the collective consciousness and mutual empowerment of these oppressed communities.) To get reacquainted with our little self, some of us will need to grieve the adulteration of our innocence and allow ourselves to be angry for what was lost or stolen from us. In this way, we must put ourselves first, especially our little selves, which is not a selfish act, but an act of self-compassion. To know true joy, we must stand in the interstices with arms wide open, accepting that both pain and pleasure are inherent to existence and, rooted in our present self, we must hold hands with our past and future selves and delight in the joy of this journey in its totality.

---

Today, connect with the playfulness of your inner child. Do your best to access a memory from your childhood where you were genuinely happy and enjoying yourself, your body, nature, friends, family, a pet, or something in the world around you. If you are having trouble remembering a specific instance, that is okay, let your imagination intervene and fill in the blanks. Gaze upon yourself with tender care, see your sweet face, listen to your voice, hear your laughter, watch your little body move. How does the little you feel and what does it feel like to open your heart to little you? Tap into self-compassion, take in the joy, and enjoy your little self. Is there anything specific you might want to express to yourself? In this moment and for the rest of this week, I want you to take a few minutes each day to engage little you, embrace your younger self and allow this part to inspire and encourage you to interact with the world from a place of childlike wonder, to see things with new eyes and a fresh perspective. Intentionally choose activities this week that allow you to pleasure in being playful—build a sandcastle, swing, splash around in the water, or finger paint. (Who knows, maybe this will become a part of your weekly routine!) As you do this, I invite you to tap into the pure joy and excitement of watching a bird take to flight, hearing the wind blow, feeling water on your skin, seeing the sun rise and set, running around the yard with a pet, dancing to your favorite song, singing at the top of your lungs, and laughing so hard your face hurts—that little kid is still (inside) you, never forget that!

## 16

## KIN-DNESS

> "Please remember, especially in these times of groupthink and the right-on chorus, that no person is your friend (or kin) who demands your silence or denies your right to grow and be perceived as fully blossomed as you were intended."
>
> — ALICE WALKER

As a young adult, I was encouraged by Christian counselors, ministers, and mentors to read books on boundaries, codependency, and cultivating a "godly self-image" and "healthy Christ-like" relationships. The pseudo-psychology touted in these texts, however, was anything but godly, Christ-like or healthy for my self-image and relationships. From twenty-one to twenty-six, I was immersed in various conversion therapies that had me convinced my sexual and emotional development had been arrested and I was in need of repair and reprogramming. (If you aren't familiar with conversion or reparative therapy, take a moment to Google or Bing it.) At the time, I felt I had no choice but to trust them and obey their instruction. In spite of my exhaustive efforts, I was no closer to being godly, healthy, or Christlike and the whole process exacerbated my abandonment and attachment issues. What I needed was not coercion, correction, and condemnation, but a safe place to explore, to love and to learn to trust myself to mature and develop the types of relationships I needed to thrive. I needed the compassion and kindness of people I chose and who chose to love me just as I am.

I left the toxic culture of a conversion-obsessed Christianity so I could save my life, literally. Over time, as I healed, I began to view myself in relation to my community and the world in concentric circles. The center is reserved for me, my Core Self—it is my inner sanctum, the core of my consciousness that is the openhearted state of my authentic being. Just outside the center is my inner circle, the three people who know me better than anyone. The subsequent circles represent the people who constitute my family, community, culture, and the larger collective of humankind. I find this imagery useful because visualizing and even understanding ourselves in terms of concentric circles can help us build and navigate healthy relationships and boundaries, regardless of our history, cultural context, or developmental trauma.

Those of us who know the pain of being rejected by our biological families, religious communities, government, and/or legal authorities or are unable to have genetic children, have had to reimagine family and create community to survive. Being queer has certainly enabled me to see the profound power of *choosing* family rather than simply *having* family, but I consider this a power and possibility available to all. We may not choose where we were born, who raised us, or how we were raised, but we can choose who we call friend or kin, and only certain friends can and should hold the honor of being our chosen family. It is a scary and difficult endeavor, which is why many of us remain in unhealthy situations—gaslit into thinking we had no alternative and/or seduced by the heteropatriarchal picture of "family" and its promise of security. To protect ourselves, we were taught to build barriers rather than boundaries, but barriers keep us bound to toxic patterns and people. Boundaries, on the other hand, afford us the opportunity to build bridges to connect with others in healthy relationships.

With experience has come emotional maturity and the ability to create better boundaries, as well as a significantly smaller inner circle. While liberating, I know how painful and prolonged this process can be; wherever you are, you are not alone. As you rebuild, I invite you to consider these three conditions, or kin-ditions (wink wink), à la Alice Walker. The people who are kin-friends: (1) never demand my silence, (2) never deny my right to grow, and (3) never dismiss my personhood. Call the people "kin" who *hear* you and encourage you to voice your truth. Call the people "kin" who *see* you and inspire you to grow emotionally, spiritually, intellectually, and physically. Call the people "kin" who *embrace* you and celebrate how you show up in the world. Shifting our understanding of family is a labor of self-compassion and kin-dness. You are no longer a passive recipient of whatever they're peddling, but an empowered agent of amity and the choice is yours.

Today, reflect upon who you consider family. While none of us has the power to decide the family into which we were born, each of us can choose who we call kin. What are your conditions and the non-negotiables you desire in your family of choice? Write them and make this affirmation, intention, and mantra: *I am free to be the only me I can be and to choose who I want to call family.*

## 17

# LIBERATION IN LOVE

"The moment we choose to love we begin to move against domination, against oppression. The moment we choose to love we begin to move towards freedom, to act in ways that liberate ourselves and others."

— BELL HOOKS

LOVE IS A CHOICE. WHILE FEAR MAY BE INSTINCTUAL, leading us to protect and preserve ourselves and our "property," love is learned and lived into, leading us to share ourselves in authenticity and open to new opportunity. Love is not synonymous with affinity or attraction, nor does it ensure comfort. While research has proven meaningful touch, genuine connection, and sexual arousal may accompany love and release oxytocin, "the love hormone," any of us with children or long-term relationships know that love entails myriad feelings and not all of them are pleasurable. According to revolutionary educator bell hooks, love is a practice that "offers no place of safety. [In love] we risk loss, hurt, pain." Sure, love may make us feel good, its great defining quality, however, is not ease, but that it is liberative, and what makes love liberative is its openness and resilience. Love elevates existence, engenders endurance, and requires responsibility if it is to flourish. Today's reflection on love is written in honor of the great bell hooks.

*Love is open, authentic, and generous.* In *All About Love*, hooks asserts, "[a] generous heart is always open, always ready to receive our going and coming. In the midst of such love, we need never fear abandonment. This is the most precious gift true love offers—the experience of knowing we always belong." In love, there is no fear because love invites us into relationship in totality and does not demand we be or become something other than who we are. While change is inevitable, when we are open to life and to love and engage in loving relationships, we need not censor parts of ourselves or ask others to curtail or closet certain characteristics. In the first stages of a relationship, we may hide what we imagine to be unsavory to promote or preserve the attachment. As we open to love, however, we gain the bravery to bring our whole selves into relationship with another—and while we are not responsible for anyone else's journey, loving and accepting ourselves fosters the same from and for others.

*Love is resilient.* Life is and always will be all the things, pleasurable, painful and everything in between. To endure and enjoy life completely, love is essential. Love is both tough and tender, firm and flexible. Love gives us the insight to accept and endure reality as well as the ability to escape abuse. hooks writes, "All too often women believe it is a sign of commitment, an expression of love, to endure unkindness or cruelty, to forgive and forget. In actuality, when we love rightly we know that the healthy, loving response to cruelty and abuse is putting ourselves out of harm's way." Love imparts fortitude and forbearance, as well as the faculty to walk the fuck away.

*Love is liberation.* Love requires responsibility, but never the ownership, control, or domination of another. Love never leads to limitation, always liberation—it sets us free. If anyone is trying to control, shame, or violate you and claiming to love you, that is not love. Love gives us the power to leave toxic relationships and to acknowledge when we are inflicting harm; this is true of individual bodies and governing bodies. If love were understood as a virtue like justice, truth, and valor, rather than a fluffy feel-good sentiment, how might diplomacy be transformed? If love informed our politics, what kind of liberation might we experience on a collective scale? Once love starts to set us free, we can't help but want the same for everyone or "to act in ways that liberate ourselves and others."

---

Today, choose to allow love to govern you on a personal and political level; after all, *the personal is political.* (Thank you, Carol Hanisch!) If choosing love means liberation rather than domination, this is a litmus test for how we live and who we allow in our life—as partners, friends, and leaders. Before you make any significant decision today (personal, professional, political, partner-related, or parental), I invite you to ask yourself this question: If love is a choice, how might love lead me now?

## 18

# MINDFULNESS IN MOVEMENT

> "Mindfulness not only makes it possible to survey our internal landscape with compassion and curiosity but can also actively steer us in the right direction for self-care."
>
> — BESSEL VAN DER KOLK

IN *THE BODY KEEPS THE SCORE*, BESSEL VAN DER KOLK writes, "the greatest source of our suffering are the lies we tell ourselves." Van der Kolk, a psychiatrist and researcher in post-traumatic stress, contends that secrets and suppression keep us at war with ourselves and trapped, feeling unsafe in the world and our bodies. True freedom, then, comes with the freedom to tell and live the truth. According to trauma researchers and clinicians like Van der Kolk, both mindfulness and movement play integral roles in liberating ourselves from the fear, judgment, and shame that keep us bound to and by lies. Acknowledging and accepting our reality is a courageous act of self-compassion that is as much about movement as it is mindfulness because it involves becoming aware of our bodies in the present moment and moving them in thoughtful and intentional ways. Mindful movement reconnects us to our bodies, which might have become unsafe for us due to trauma. It relieves stress, expresses emotion, and releases pent-up energy, which calms our nervous system and provides a safe place from which to process traumatic memories.

The word trauma comes from the Greek word τραῦμᾰ, which means "wound," and has evolved in connotation and application over the past four centuries. While the notion was first included in the DSM in 1952 (PTSD appeared in 1980) and Van der Kolk published his book in 2014, it was during the global pandemic that "trauma" became a household word, which is also when *The Body Keeps the Score* made it to the *New York Times* Best Seller list. Trauma is any event that causes physical, emotional, or psychological distress, but trauma varies in degree (which is why some use "t" and "T" to differentiate) and not all of us respond to trauma in the same way. Trauma-informed research has revealed that a trauma is never just a one-time occurrence because it leaves an imprint. A traumatic event in the past becomes a very present reality by embedding in our mind, brain, and body. In this way, trauma can lead to the reorganization of our brain as well as our lives and can inhibit us from movement, both literally and figuratively; this is especially true when we are triggered or activated by a trauma stimulus.

While trauma and any subsequent fear can keep us frozen in potentially destructive patterns, mindfulness offers a compassionate way to get unstuck. Near the end of the twentieth century, neuroscience began demonstrating that we are not victims of circumstance and can change the way we feel. Through various studies they proved that the brain's neuroplasticity allows us to rewire neural pathways that have developed over time, but this restructuring can only happen when we become aware of and befriend what is happening inside us. Our inner experience is cognitive, emotional, and physiological. Therefore, before we can transform the way we think or feel, we must understand the relationship of cognition to embodiment—how we think and what we feel are intimately interconnected.

I cannot recall the first time I heard the phrase "mind over matter," but I heard it often and from some very influential adults. Western European society, a literary cultural, overemphasizes and even glorifies the cerebral to the detriment of our physical and emotional bodies and their interdependence. The hallmark of Western philosophy and, therefore, the traditional understanding of ourselves as humans can be summed up in René Descartes' famous assertion, "I think, therefore, I am." While Descartes indubitably honored the relationship of mind to body, the unfortunate legacy of *cogito ergo sum* is the elevation of the rational and the disparaging of the emotional. (Many of us are well-acquainted with the devastating effects of the dichotomizing and gendering of these concepts, i.e., the "rational" has been equated with the male/masculine and the emotional with the [irrational] female/feminine.) The very word deployed to describe emotions, "feelings," indicates where emotions happen and highlights the mind-body connection; emotions occur in our bodies and brains, affecting the entirety of our being. Oral and non-Western cultures honor this relationship as evinced in their integrative approaches to healing, medicine, and movement. Rather than assuming that thinking is reliable, and our feelings cannot be trusted, what if we pay attention to our emotions, feel them, and let them guide us to better understand ourselves, the relationship of our mind and body, and how we might heal? Afterall, the word "emotion" comes from the Latin word *emovere*, which means to "move," "stir up," or "move out."

Mindful movement is a form of medicine *from* our bodies, *for* our bodies. While some of us legitimately require medication for homeostasis, as a culture we have become so accustomed to taking medicine for ailments that many of us never learn our body's rhythms, automatic processes, or its capacity to heal itself. Movement is a way the body relieves tension and stress to bring us into harmony. Exercise stimulates the body to emit neurotransmitters; the endorphins, dopamine, and endocannabinoids secreted generate feelings of well-being that contribute to mental health and emotional regulation. Aerobic activities like walking, running, dancing, biking, surfing, paddling, and pickleball release endorphins, which give us a short-lived euphoric state that can stay with us hours after we take off our trainers. Of course, if these activities are not available to you and your body, there are gentler ways to move your that are just as beneficial — yoga, stretching, tai chi, and water aerobics are wonderful examples. I encourage you to find what is appropriate and accessible to you; even dancing, swaying, or rocking in a chair can also help soothe and regulate your nervous system. When we are mindful about how we move our bodies, we cultivate a space for mind and body to reconnect, release helpful chemicals into our bloodstream, and dislodge feelings trapped in our bodies. Mindful movement disrupts the socially constructed division between body and mind, which has contributed to our disintegration and disembodiment, and facilitates our healing.

---

Today, move your body mindfully in a way that aligns with your unique physique and ability. Physical movement brings us into the moment and the rhythm of our body can serve to liberate and recalibrate us. When our attention rests and moves with the body, we become present, even playful, and intrusive thoughts and painful emotions have less room to overwhelm us or pull us into worry or agitation. It is not that we are avoiding our pain, but that we are acknowledging our pain and intentionally utilizing our bodies as a tool for release. As you move your body, notice how it feels. It need not be strenuous and should not cause pain. Keep it as simple as you need. In this restful dynamic state, become the movement and enjoy the peaceful connection of body and mind.

# NURTURE THROUGH NONJUDGMENT AND NONABANDONMENT

"Sometimes being brave requires letting the crowd think you're a coward. Sometimes being brave means letting everyone down but yourself."

— GLENNON DOYLE

MANY OF US BEGIN THE JOURNEY TOWARD SELF-LOVE searching for something we did not receive in childhood. Each of us has been let down and can understand the ache of abandonment, whether through the rejection of a parent/caretaker, the anguish of unrequited love, or the pain of being denied something important. In her book, *Self-Compassion*, Dr. Kristin Neff elucidates the three elements of self-compassion. Today, I will offer a summary of these essential components and guide you through a practical application of this triad.

The first aspect of self-compassion is mindfulness and involves both the awareness *that* we are suffering and the validation *of* our suffering. Mindfulness means we are conscious of and open to our experience, allowing sensations, thoughts, and emotions to surface without judgment or evasion. Most of us have been trained to label events and our reactions to them as "good" or "bad" and to embrace the former and avoid the latter, since we are hardwired to avoid pain. As a result, it is counterintuitive to simply be aware and allow ourselves the freedom to have a challenging experience, respond to it, and seek to understand and validate that response. In cultures where showing and even having emotion is a sign of weakness, accepting, understanding, and validating feelings poses a threat to the social order. It is much easier, then, to talk ourselves out of an emotion than to pause, acknowledge what is happening, and hold space for it. This is often the case because many of us learned to relate to emotions through overidentification. To heal, we must not only allow ourselves to feel emotions, instead of judging and suppressing them, but also refrain from overidentifying with them. An example of this critical difference is found in the distinction between the statements, "I am suffering because I failed" versus "I am a failure." The aspiration here is to have and hold the experience with awareness rather than be completely absorbed so as to be defined by it or permit it to perpetuate a self-deprecating narrative. Mindfulness endows us with the facility to feel sad when we fail and not label ourselves a failure because of it.

The second component of self-compassion is common humanity and is defined by acknowledging that suffering inheres in the human condition and, therefore, connects us all. As psychologist Tara Brach points out, pain often leads us to isolate in the "trance of unworthiness," overcome by shame and fear. Rather than dividing us, however, just like flaws and failures, pain should unite us because it is universal. If we can acknowledge that all humans have flaws, fail, feel pain, and are in-progress, we can let ourselves off the hook and tap into a larger network of support—trading radical individualism for radical (self)compassion. (Self)Compassion shatters the perception of ourselves as individuals, disconnected from the whole or outside the human experience; it frees us from the compulsion to protect our ego from an unpredictable event or unknowable other, so we can settle into ourselves.

The third, and final, component of self-compassion is self-kindness. We have become accustomed to chastising our shortcomings and judging ourselves when we struggle, but Neff invites us to consider how we might treat a suffering lover, child, or friend. What would you say? Would you critique or condemn or offer a compassionate touch or loving embrace? The experience of suffering grants us the opportunity to meet ourselves with gentleness, ask ourselves the most compassionate question—*What do you need?* —and respond in care.

---

Today, nurture yourself through nonjudgment and nonabandonment. Even as the nurse must provide nonjudgmental care and the physician has an obligation of nonabandonment, make these vows to yourself today. Call upon your wisest, truest, and most loving self. From this place, sit with the smaller, scared, insecure part of you. When you are ready, ask the following question:

What do you need and how might I offer you that in this moment? Allow yourself to respond, stay present with yourself, and give yourself just what you need without judgment. Whether a soothing word or phrase, a loving touch, or the space to express, emote, or move your body, nurture yourself freely and completely today.

## 20

# OPENNESS

"Ego is like a room of your own, a room with a view, with the temperature and the smells and the music that you like. You want it your own way. You'd just like to have a little peace; you'd just like to have a little happiness, you know, just 'gimme a break!' But the more you think that way, the more you will try to get life to come out so that it will always suit you, the more your fear of other people and what's outside your room grows. Rather than becoming more relaxed, you start pulling down the shades and locking the door. When you do go out, you find the experience more and more unsettling and disagreeable. You become touchier, more fearful, more irritable than ever. The more you just try to get it your way, the less you feel at home. To begin to develop compassion for yourself and others, you have to unlock the door. You don't open it yet, because you have to work with your fear that somebody you don't like might come in. Then as you begin to relax and befriend those feelings, you begin to open it."

— PEMA CHÖDRÖN

No one really knows the purpose of life, but I am sure it's not getting everything just the way we want it. Doing that would result in expending most of our energy trying to create the perfect conditions and whatever is left would be spent coping with our inevitable disappointment, since such conditions cannot be sustained. It has been said that the only constant in life is change and the only thing that is certain is uncertainty, which is why teachers like Pema Chödrön encourage us to get comfortable with uncertainty. In Chödrön's description of this predicament, after we open the door of the room that is our ego, we can expect discomfort and disagreement to emerge. Once we open ourselves in this way, however, our various visitors provide opportunities to expand our compassion by connecting with the tenderness of our experience and our emotions.

Chödrön tells a story about the spiritual teacher Gurdjieff, who invited an ill-tempered man into his community. No one could stand this guy because of his awful attitude. It seemed that everything irritated him, and he would throw a tantrum every time he was perturbed. One day, as the story goes, Gurdjieff had his students doing a mundane task as a spiritual exercise. The chore was so tedious that the cantankerous man got fed up and fled the property. His departure led to spontaneous relief and revelry for the others, but Gurdjieff tracked him down and brought him back. When asked why he did so, Gurdjieff responded with confidence and a glint in his eye, "I pay him to be here."

Most of us who are Americans have been conditioned to believe we should not be inconvenienced, so we become offended when our lives are interrupted. This is an inherently privileged perspective that is unrealistic and has led many of us to significant frustration and anxiety and has contributed to great internal and external conflict. We spend so much of our time resisting and rejecting our current experience in favor of some inaccessible ideal that few of us have come to acknowledge the intrinsic uncertainty of life. Life is unpredictable, and inconvenience is an unavoidable aspect of existence. As such, rather than a source of angst, we could reframe uncertainty as an invitation to growth, flexibility, and equanimity as well as an opportunity to open rather than shut down. What we resist persists, but what we see has the capacity to set us free if we can name and reframe our experience.

---

Today, recall something you find mildly irritating—no need to find the most annoying thing. This is a first step, so be gentle. Why do you find this person, thing, or situation to be so aggravating? If you chose not to label it negatively or interpret it as irksome, how else might you understand it? Could it serve to teach or offer you something? If nothing else, might it invite you to check in with yourself, get curious about the trigger, and choose to come back to your Core Self in compassion and openness rather than be pulled into a place of anxiety and agitation?

## 21

# PURPOSE & POISE

> "With wisdom, we do not see ourselves as a master or ruler of the world in any way. Rather, we see ourselves as part of the world, an interconnected and interdependent systemic whole."
>
> — SUNITA RAI

THE CULTURES WITH THE GREATEST LONGEVITY AND quality of life, Dan Buettner's "blue zones," are those where people are most connected to their purpose, well-being, community, and ecosystem. While there is one blue zone in the US and our fitness industry is booming, as a culture, America does not support the sustenance of a healthy integrated lifestyle for all. In fact, like most Western societies, research reveals Americans live a rather stratified and disembodied existence, paying little attention to the relationship of class to health or the physical body to the psyche and emotional body. In today's reflection on purpose—our reason for living—and the poise, or balance, required to be *in* our purpose,

I offer four concepts from other cultures' wisdom traditions. Each of these words has no English equivalent and every single one, in its own way, honors the interdependence of mind and body as well as that of humanity and the environment. In Japanese, we find the term *ikigai*, often rendered, "that which gives life purpose." The second, *ubuntu* (or *umuntu*), from Zulu and the Bantu languages of Southern Africa, is roughly translated, "I am, because you are," and represents compassion and/in the interconnectedness of humanity. In Tibetan, the word *tonglen* means "to give and receive in compassion" and, in Chinese, the term *wu wei* signifies "to be in flow."

Attempting to translate any of these terms directly into English is difficult because there is no single English word that encapsulates any one of these ideas. For example, various Westerners have translated *ikigai* as one's reason for being, employing a Venn diagram to attempt to convey *ikigai* as the intersection of one's passion, mission, vocation, and profession. Unfortunately, this cannot adequately represent *ikigai*, which assumes fluidity and change over time—even as we are meant to grow as humans, so, too, what gives our life purpose is ever evolving. It appears that *ikigai*, like *ubuntu*, *tonglen*, and *we wei*, is more expansive than any one English word because these concepts speak to a fundamental difference in cultural values and wisdom. The semantic range of *ikigai*, for instance, appears to make room for human growth throughout the stages of life. In American culture, people are expected to pick one career, "master" it, and are rewarded for their commitment; such a paradigm gives little care or consideration to the twists and turns, transitions and transformations inherent to human existence. American culture gives precedence to individuality and uniqueness, Southern African cultures, on the other hand, prioritizes the implicit interdependence of humanity. While the term "interdependence" conveys mutuality, *ubuntu* represents a philosophy of life that honors the individual as integral to and contingent upon the community. *Ubuntu* expresses not just a particular collective consciousness but the consciousness of the collective such that there is no "me" without a "we." *Tonglen* and *wu wei*, for their part, signify interconnectedness and equilibrium in Tibetan Buddhism and Daoist philosophy respectively—the former through compassionate reciprocity and the latter by inexertion or not forcing, allowing for the natural flow and balance of life. Focusing on ourselves as solitary individuals, "masters" of a single occupation that is our sole purpose, is an inherently imbalanced approach to life that has led many of us to mental and physical illness. Alternatively, as we prioritize balance—of our biological rhythms and within our ecosystem—we come to access and amplify our power, purpose, and poise.

---

Today, consider the twists and turns your life has taken. Settle into your seat, feet on the ground, hands in your lap, and imagine you are an oak tree with the wisdom of centuries. Visualize your roots expanding, reaching deep into the earth and grounding you. Now, see your branches reaching up to the sky, bearing fruit and sheltering life. From here, feel your connection to all life and reconsider your purpose from this poised state of equanimity.

## 22

# THE POWER OF PRESENCE

"Past and future are in the mind only—I am now."

— SRI NISARGADATTA MAHARAJ

THE ONLY MOMENT IN WHICH WE TRULY HAVE POWER IS the present. We could spend time and energy regretting what happened yesterday or five years ago, we might worry about tomorrow or where we'll be in a decade, but the only moment in which we truly have power is the present. Eckart Tolle frames it in this way, "Nothing has happened in the past; it happened in the Now. Nothing will ever happen in the future; it will happen in the Now." Yes, it is responsible to learn from the past and we must make decisions for our future, but regret and worry rob us of the power of being present in and to this present moment. The key to unlocking that power is in recognizing we always have a choice where to place our attention and intention.

The average human has around 60,000 thoughts per

day; of those, at least 30,000 are wandering. In other words, we spend half of our time thinking about things with no real point or purpose. Now, I am not suggesting that our thought life must always have a point or purpose. Daydreaming can be quite generative and allowing our minds to wander and to wonder gives us a break from the demands of adulting, and can aid us in productivity, emotional processing, and the alleviation (or at least reduction) of anxiety. If half of our day is spent mentally meandering, however, most of us spend 50 to 75% of that time in worry—particularly if we parent, own a business, or are responsible in some capacity for other lives. What if there was a way to make our thought life more efficient and, in so doing, make life more enjoyable?

Transforming our relationship with the present through the power of presence is an expression of self-love and an exercise in self-compassion. As we become more aware of our experience in the now, we become more available to ourselves and those around us. There may be no greater form of compassion than being radically present to what is happening *in the present*. If the root of suffering (*dukkha*), according to Buddhist philosophy, is craving (*tanha*). Then, each time we attempt to cling to what we label "good" and reject what we judge to be "bad," we create suffering. Happiness and joy are byproducts of serenity, a state of calm accessed through openhearted acceptance of life as it is. Dissatisfaction and disappointment result from our attempts to fight, fix, or flee from circumstances outside our control. When we cease trying to force favorable outcomes, accept the conditions we cannot control, and allow the present moment to be as it is, we find ourselves in flow or "in the zone"—fully present, focused, and joyful.

To be clear, it is possible to advocate for human rights and against injustice, while also accepting the present moment as it is; the two things may appear contradictory, but are, in fact, in alignment. Acceptance is not apathy. When I accept this moment, who I am in it, and the power I have, I can move toward being more conscious, connected, and compassionate. Accepting the present moment does not mean consenting to unjust systems of power or inequitable power dynamics and is not the same as accommodation or acquiescence. Radical acceptance is knowing who I am and activating the power of my presence in the present moment and milieu. It is not idly sitting, but actively engaging in the world. I can accept the present and, at the same time, hold others and myself accountable to radical compassion.

---

Today, reflect on The Serenity Prayer: "Grant me the serenity to accept the things I cannot change, the courage to change the things I can, and the wisdom to know the difference." Now, take this moment and choose to be present to the world around you through your 5 senses—see 5 things, hear 4 things, feel 3 things, smell 2 things, and taste 1 thing. Staying radically present to your power and the power of your presence is today's act of self-compassion.

## QUEER(Y)ING

"Be patient towards all that is unsolved in your heart and try to love the questions themselves. Live the questions now. Perhaps you will then gradually, without noticing it, live along some distant day into the answer."

— RAINIER MARIA RILKE

When I was a professor of religion and philosophy, students often asked life's most perplexing existential quandaries. Behind every glimmering eye and inquiring mind was hope for an answer or some semblance of certainty. Much to their chagrin, time and again, I would "answer" with a question. Instead of solidifying certitude, I invited them into the open space of exploration and investigation; not to mention there is very little about this wondrous world we can know for sure. Just as Rilke's young poet, I wanted my students to live the questions and possibly, eventually, access serenity instead of certainty—finding peace in the process rather than a destination. The quest *for* certainty may appear benign but is as hazardous as the claim *of* certainty. Arising from the egoic hunger for possession and power over, certainty confines us to cognitive rigidity, oversimplification, and polarization. Querying, alternatively, is a quest for understanding, leading us to a more tender place, promoting creativity, connection, and collaboration rather than individualism, opposition, and alienation.

The quest for certainty condemns us to conformity and while conformity has advantages for survival, those of us for whom normative ways of thinking and being do not come "naturally" have, nonetheless, found other ways to survive. I consider the means through which we have done so to have endowed us with select superpowers, like observing society and its systems from the periphery. In this way, one might say we have a birds' eye, or maybe even God's eye, view. Due to our queer positionality as perpetual participant observers, we are curious, creative, and well-equipped to coach normies in rethinking reality. Another of our superpowers is empowering people to pose questions they might not otherwise ask and inspiring them to live into queries they might not otherwise pursue. Here is an example dear to me:

My partner spent over half her life in cis-gender heterosexual relationships. She'd always found women attractive but had no access to the socialization or support system she needed to seek out and sustain a same-gender loving relationship. In addition, she had qualms about the way society functioned and how knowledge was produced and policed, but such inquisitiveness was not encouraged in her context. The more she cultivated the curiosity and courage of her Core Self, and connected with BIPOC and queer people, the less she required the certainty of traditional psychosocial structures. Embracing herself and her que(e)ries, led her to manifest superpowers and a healthy loving queer relationship that supports her search for authenticity and integration.

Albert Einstein once said, "One cannot help but be in awe when [contemplating] the mysteries of eternity, of life, of the marvelous structure of reality. It is enough if one tries merely to comprehend a little of this mystery every day. Never lose a holy curiosity." Queerying is a holy queer exercise in curiosity, courage, and compassion and a way we worship through wondering about existence in this complex cosmos. Queerying is an expression of love aiding us in marveling at life's mysteries revealed in our diverse ways of thinking and being.

---

Today, connect with your deepest queries about life, love, loss, and the lessons you've learned. Write down as many as you can. Take a moment to wonder what you might do, see, or be if you lived into your questions. Rather than giving into (legitimate) fear about what you don't know or can't control in life, I invite you to make a choice to marvel at the mysteries of life and, if just for a moment, feel into the freedom of allowing yourself to be all (and in whatever way) you want to be. May your queries become a catalyst for compassion and a catapult into courageous action.

## 24

## REST FOR RENEWAL

"Perhaps the earth can teach us, as when everything seems dead and later proves to be alive."

— PABLO NERUDA

IT WOULD DO US GREAT GOOD, AS MEMBERS OF THE so-called animal kingdom, to learn from the earth and other organisms. As a species, humans have done great damage to establish our dominance and distance ourselves from our creatureliness. Sir Charles Lyell's notion of "mind over matter" has been misinterpreted in myriad ways to rationalize (quite literally) the dominance of the human mind over our bodies and others. With the threat of climate change and the extinction of 15,000 species, however, the Earth's ecosystem and our creaturely cohabitants clamor for our attention and our action. We, humans, have so much to learn from our precious planet and the life cycles we have so aggressively disrupted, particularly about rest and renewal. What if, instead of having *dominion over* the planet, we enjoyed compassionate *communion with* it? How might this affect our planetary community? Could we save our planet and possibly ourselves?

Humanity's relationship to the earth and its diverse species has historically entailed fear. While the natural world can be chaotic, I believe humanity has proven itself far more dangerous. Rather than honoring unpredictability as a fact of life, humans have repeatedly sought to assert authority over it; exploiting our planet for enjoyment, entertainment, and economic advantage—humans have mistreated other humans, animals, natural resources, as well as the cycles of our physical and emotional bodies. The inclination toward domination, and its justification, can also be seen in our interaction with textual bodies, like the Bible. (Even the non-religious among us experience the Bible's influence via Western European imperial expansion and the colonization of 80% of the planet.) Genesis 1:28 is exemplary in this regard, deployed to justify Man's divine right to Master, this passage could be interpreted otherwise. As a product of oral cultures, the Bible is a compilation of stories meant to be read symbolically, whose authors and redactors prioritized their interests veiled as God's will (since some believe[d] them to be synonymous). In Ancient Hebrew, many words have several meanings, so transcribers made calculated decisions, and in Genesis 1:28, *radah*, translated "have dominion," could have been transcribed "steward"—one who "looks after, cares for." Just as fear need not necessitate force, power need not imply oppression. A more compassionate approach to dominion is communion, requiring us to listen and learn—just because a body does not speak a language intelligible to us doesn't mean it's got nothing to say or teach us.

Instead of listening to the various bodies (animal, geographical, celestial, and even textual) communicating with us and offering wisdom, we have perpetually sought to colonize and control them—having been conditioned to conquer unruly bodies rather than compassionately commune with them. "Mind over matter" as a framework for life is antithetical to mental health and holistic wellness because it compels us to push through or anesthetize physical and emotional pain, disregarding all bodies' need for rest(oration) and renewal. Whole-health educator Therese Jornlin advises we trust the body's intelligence and honor its cycles. Tiredness, heaviness, even depression, according to Jornlin, are not cause for frustration and force, but invitations to relaxation. The compassionate response, then, is to care for our bodies as they care for us. Just like the four seasons and the stages of all life, our energy, productivity, and excitement will continually wax and wane. When we commune with rather than attempt to dominate ourselves and our environment, we find our greatest power is not in distrusting or disrupting life's cycles, but in their preservation—listening and learning how to live from other life on this planet. The earth is perpetually in a cycle of regeneration, we are meant for the same.

---

Today, listen to your body. What is it saying and what does it need? In what ways has the mantra "mind over matter" inhibited you from listening to what you and your body need? What might it look like to give yourself the gift of rest for your renewal today? Our bodies send us signals, warning lights to help us care for and maintain them. If you feel agitated, take a break, go for a walk, and give that nervous energy an outlet. If you feel overwhelmed, offer yourself a moment to breathe, meditate, and self-regulate. If you feel exhausted, allow yourself time for repose and re-creation. As you live, love, and listen to your body and others, you will gradually be led into a fuller and more fulfilling life. Now, if you feel comfortable, repeat the following mantra to yourself as many times as you like throughout the day: *May I be happy. May I be healthy. May I be at peace.*

## 25

# SELF-CARE AS SELF-PRESERVATION AND SELF-DETERMINATION

"Caring for myself is not self-indulgence. It is self-preservation, and that is an act of political warfare."

— AUDRE LORDE

IF YOU HAVE BECOME AVERSE TO THE TERM "SELF-CARE" because of its overuse, you are not alone. Self-care has become hackneyed and has deviated substantially from its original use by the likes of Angela Davis and Audre Lorde. The semantic range of the word is so diffuse now, it includes anything from meditation and meal prep to spa days and skin care routines. A term that was originally deployed for Black queer and feminist liberation, self-determination, and communal consolidation—as these iconoclasts cared for themselves through mindfulness and healthy habits that promoted their overall well-being—has been co-opted by white capitalists to perpetuate individualism, justify excess, and promote profiteering on the heels of a global pandemic.

Lovingkindness teacher Sharon Salzberg highlights the distinction between selfishness, or egoism, and the self-love that motivates us to genuine self-care: "This kind of compulsive concern with 'I, me, and mine' isn't the same as loving ourselves...Loving ourselves points us to capacities of resilience, compassion, and understanding within that are simply part of being alive." I appreciate Salzberg's reflections, *and* I believe that, like the Body Positivity Movement, we should look to the Black feminists and womanists whose resilience, compassion, and understanding teaches us to not take these privileges for granted. These enlightened and indomitable icons realized that to stay alive and to thrive they had to create a new way for themselves to be human; for them, self-care was, and still is, self-determination and self-determination was, and always will be, self-care.

Whatever your understanding of or feelings about self-care, Audre Lorde's words can ground us in understanding caring acts toward ourselves as labors of self-love, personal empowerment, and activism—particularly those of us led to believe we do not deserve or cannot afford to care for ourselves. As "a Black, lesbian, mother, warrior, poet," Lorde lived at the intersections of oppression in our heteropatriarchal white supremacist society. As she saw it, any effort made toward self-determination and self-affirmation was at odds with the dominant cultural narrative, which privileges white, hetero, cis, male, abled, Christian, upper class American citizens above all other lives, and I agree. Those of us who are BIPOC, women, LGBTQ+, neurodiverse, lower class, non-Christian, immigrants, and/or are living with a disability must work twice as hard. Those of us, who like Lorde, embody multiple and intersecting marginalized identities must work three to four times harder, even as white men absorb most of the wealth in the United States. (As of 2023, white households were at least six times wealthier than Black—a result of white supremacist economic policies that ensure the generational wealth of whites.) This is not to say white people or men do not also deserve the right to care for themselves, but that the rest of us have not been caring for ourselves *in order to care for him* and this must stop. Through her representation of self-care as a political act, Audre Lorde not only empowered Black women, she incited a revolution that inverts the traditional hierarchies of Western culture, so those who have historically been dehumanized become the agents of their preservation and prioritization.

Recording artist Janelle Monáe once said, "I'm nonbinary, so I just don't see myself as a woman ... solely. I feel like God is so much bigger than the he or the she. And if I am from God, I am everything...Even if it makes others uncomfortable, I will love who I am." For a society that has historically disrespected, even denied, the personhood of BIPOC and LGBTQ+ persons, to love yourself is an act of resistance and a revolutionary feat with the power to reform and transform our world. It is vital that we acknowledge the reality that those of us who exist in marginalized communities and embody non-normative identities experience great trauma to our central nervous systems daily, which is what makes self-care an act of self-preservation—it is a matter of life and death. The expression and extent of the trauma may vary between us, but our suffering is real and can lead to solidarity between communities and across racial, cultural, and religious lines. It is time we love ourselves, *even if it makes others uncomfortable*, by prioritizing our mental health and well-being, so that we become champions of self-compassion for ourselves and one another.

---

Today, find an activity you can do to prioritize yourself and practice compassionate self-care. Do you want to start meditating? Try a yoga class? Journal for 15 minutes a day? How about read a few pages from a self-compassion book each morning—you are already doing that now, way to go! Once you have found something that is revitalizing for you, I invite you make a commitment to implement this practice daily, so it becomes part of your routine. (You could even continue to use this book after the first thirty days—repetition moves information from our brains to our bodies and transforms knowledge into wisdom.)

26

# SYMPATHY TOWARD SOLIDARITY

"Nobody's free until everybody's free."

— FANNIE LOU HAMER

THE QUESTION I WAS ASKED MOST AS A PROFESSOR WAS twofold: "Do you believe in universal truth and how do you know which truths are universal?" My response was always the same and, of course, included a question: "Look at the world's religions, which teachings are shared? This gets us as close as possible to universal truth; where we find resonance, we find reliability." I will not recite all the truths I have found through the years, but I will identify what I consider the most important: The Golden Rule. In the Qur'an, it is, "Do unto all as you would wish to have done unto you; and reject for others what you would reject for yourself." According to the Buddha, "What is disagreeable to yourself, do not do to others." In the words of Confucius, "Do not do to others what you do not want them to do to you," and for

Jesus, a Palestinian Jew, it was the greatest commandment: love your neighbor as yourself.

Each of these teachings conveys an ethic of reciprocity, rooted in sympathy. Sympathy derives from a Greek word that literally means "feeling with." While empathy represents being *in* (*em-*) someone's feeling or suffering, sympathy represents being *affected by* someone else's feeling or experience. (These two English words are distinguished at times by authors, like Brene Brown, who understand the former to foster connection whereas they perceive the latter, like pity, to stem from a sense of superiority and, thereby, create separation.) Regardless of how we might define or differentiate the two, we cannot begin to want *for* others what we want for ourselves until we feel *with* them. Feeling *with* enables us to see others, even the most different and difficult, as equals with needs and rights as important as ours. In feeling *with*, "the other" is no longer an abstract concept or inconsequential entity—to disdain or keep at a distance—but someone we allow into our hearts. Sympathy, then, is not a barrier, but a gateway to empathy and compassion; to not just feel, but to *suffer with* and so be moved to compassionate action.

Pema Chödrön frames compassion not as a relationship between healer and wounded but between equals, offering insight into the essence of solidarity as suffering *with*. She writes, "Only when we know our own darkness well can we be present with the darkness of others. Compassion becomes real when we recognize our shared humanity." Solidarity, like compassion, is contingent upon connecting with our own tender heart in recognition of our shared humanity. When we hold space for *all* our experiences and emotions, we can do the same for others. As we feel with and for ourselves, we have the capacity to feel with and for others. Then, we can embrace others in their suffering, stand with them in their struggles, and seek their emancipation and empowerment. Sympathy is a muscle we exercise, strengthened as we feel and are moved to act. Becoming aware of our shared humanity leads us to honor our differences, to see and stand with others, which is the essence of solidarity. When we truly live in self-compassion our purpose becomes collective liberation because we know in our bones "nobody's free until everybody's free."

---

Today, think of someone very unlike you; they may look or sound different, hold different values or political views. Choose a person who hasn't violated a boundary —self-love is manifest in building the muscle of sympathy *and* in creating boundaries when someone has hurt you. Now, consider what you have in common— even if it is you are human and experience suffering. (Based on our DNA, all humans 99.9% similar!) Fix your attention on any similarities you can think of and ways they might have suffered in their life. As you have learned to hold space for your pain, fear, and worries, know they have those same experiences too. I invite you to extend compassion to yourself and, when you are ready, to offer them compassion. If there is no difference between loving yourself and loving another, any effort to sympathize with another person's experience and offer them compassion is an act of solidarity and a labor of self-love.

## WHOLEHEARTEDNESS

*"Love is or it ain't. Thin love ain't love at all."*

— TONI MORRISON

THOSE OF US WHO ARE NOT WHITE, CIS-GENDER, straight men in America were trained to doubt and diminish ourselves and our abilities. It is not that white men do not struggle with insecurity or self-doubt—they most certainly do—but that the rest of us have been culturally conditioned to understand ourselves as accessories and/or auxiliary to "the Man." Even as we were taught to take up less space, our white male counterparts were encouraged to spread their wings, and their legs, and take up as much of the land, government, office, room, and bed as they wanted and felt they deserved. Ironically, as white men have gained more and more public and political power, their mental health and emotional well-being has suffered grievously because to "be a man" has entailed rejecting and repressing what makes them most human. This systemic suppression has had catastrophic repercussions for the rest of humanity as well as our ecosystem; the prevalence and endurance of racism, sexism, misogyny, xenophobia, and ecocide are evidence. To create the conditions for our healing we must first acknowledge the totality of this systematic obstruction and the reality that *all of us* are inhibited from inhabiting our full selves and, as a result, *all of us* are suffering. When any part of our population is programmed to perceive themselves as inferior, we all suffer and lose sight of our significance and our sentience; if any of us is subordinated, none of us is liberated. Compassion has fueled every effective social justice movement and undergirded efforts toward the abolition of all manner of oppressive institutions. Compassion creates the conditions for our healing because love alone can liberate us to live wholeheartedly. This entry is dedicated to all of us who were told anytime that any part of us was too much: too much excitement, too much emotion, too much energy, too much enjoyment, too much intensity, too much too-muchness. It is time to love yourself big and right back to wholeheartedness.

A distinguishing feature of love is that it never asks you to shrink yourself in any way. Love never demands you get small or silent and it never pressures you to betray yourself or your body. Love does not yell at you to sit down, shut up, and it certainly doesn't demand you stop crying. Fear, love's shadow, is the voice that tells us to get tiny and to accept living in terror. Fear is timid and treacherous, but love is tenacious and trustworthy. Love is confident in the face of fear's confusion. When fear is anxious and impulsive, love shows up as firm and forbearing. Even as fear cowers behind criticism and contentiousness, love remains courageous and compassionate. Love maintains healthy boundaries, yet it is *all in* because it knows and honors *all it is*, and because love respects itself, it does not have to protect itself nor does it need to withhold affection. Fear is half-hearted, but love is always already one hundred percent wholehearted.

Lots of us hold back because we are afraid of losing control or being rejected, since we were led to believe we are not welcome or wanted in our totality. For many of us, humanity has been inhospitable and the hurt we harbor has yet to heal. If someone shames or abuses you and leads you to believe you are inferior and/or at fault, they are operating out of fear, not love, and it is time to leave or find the assistance you need to remove yourself safely from that unhealthy dynamic. (For support, please see the list of helplines in the Appendix.) When we make self-compassion a practice, we grow to wholeheartedly embrace ourselves and can put our whole selves into whatever we do without fear of rejection or negative repercussions; this is real love. The next time you find yourself in a bind and do not know where to turn or what to do, sit in tender self-compassion and ask yourself the following: What would love want (for me)? How would love respond to this situation? What would love say or do in this moment? Let love lead and see where it takes you...

---

Today, I invite you to respond to the following prompt. Let yourself flow, stream of consciousness, without holding back. Give this gift to yourself and return to this piece and practice once a month as a personal check-in and act of self-compassion. Prompt: What if you only had one week to live? What would you do? Where would you go? With whom would you spend time? Is there anything you need to get off your chest? Is there a certain plan or desire you want to put into action? What, if anything, is holding you back? Is there something or someone preventing you from doing, saying, or being what you want? Who and why? Is it time to create an exit strategy? Today might be the day to do so. Regardless, it is always the day to sit and reflect in self-compassion. Real love is wholehearted, it goes all the way in, all the way down, and all the way through with what it wants to do. Take this time to love you.

# XENOPHOBIA

"No one is born hating another person because of the color of skin, background, or religion. People must learn to hate, and if they can learn to hate, they can be taught to love, for love comes more naturally to the human heart than its opposite."

— NELSON MANDELA

XENOPHOBIA IS PREJUDICE AGAINST PEOPLE FROM another race or ethnicity. Deriving from the Greek words ξένος, "foreign, strange," and φόβος, "fear," a more literal translation is "fear of what is foreign." This translation offers insight into the correlation between fear and prejudice as well as the genesis of hate. Like fear, prejudice and hatred have a source. None of our emotions or attitudes develop in a vacuum, they are the result of social conditioning and external stimuli and are, quite often, inextricably and unwittingly linked to our survival. Unfortunately, rather than evolving to be curious about, befriend, and even overcome what frightens us about the unfamiliar, many of us make assumptions and develop aversions. When such aversions ossify over time, they manifest in xenophobic biases rather than compassionate engagement. Today, we are going to work with this type of fear to see if we can breathe a little life into what might have become petrified.

Fear is a primary, or core, emotion directly tied to our limbic system. Here, we find the so-called fear center of our brain, the amygdala, which has also been deemed "the reptilian brain" because all vertebrates, even reptiles, have this fight-or-flight fear response system. Fear of threat is a functional experience common to all animals. Not all animals, however, perceive unfamiliarity as a threat and not all humans see new people, places, or experiences as threatening. So, while fear of what is foreign is a survival trait, it is not a trait necessary for survival, which is precisely why we can evolve beyond xenophobia. Xenophobia is a fear of what is foreign that metastasizes into prejudice against it. Prejudice and hatred toward what is foreign can certainly be understood as functional—because they can be coping mechanisms deployed to protect individuals and in-groups from real or perceived threat—but neither prejudice nor hatred inhere in humans like fear. We have no "hate center" in our brains, and prejudices are based on socialization and biases that stem from a myopic understanding of identity, in-groups, and outgroups. Xenophobia, the menacing combination of prejudice and hatred toward what is foreign, is learned; and, as Nelson Mandela asserts, as easy as it is to hate what we don't know, hate does not come as naturally to us as love.

Considering xenophobia in light of history is instructive here. As civilizations dispersed and engaged one another, stories abounded about real and imagined "others." Of the documents that have survived we find narratives expressing and evoking fear of contamination, corruption, and complete cultural collapse, which quite often resulted in conflict and campaigns to control, colonize, and ethnically cleanse. Through the evolution of our species and the frontotemporal lobe, humans developed empathy alongside executive function, enabling us to respond logically and considerately rather than simply to react in fear when confronted with difference. Rather than simply avoiding or eradicating what was foreign, we learned to communicate and cooperate across linguistic, ethnic, and cultural boundaries, establishing treaties, building alliances, and creating coalitions to exchange goods and ideas. Humans even organized organizations to protect and promote peace, human rights, and environmental stewardship. (Unfortunately, though the system is in place, the process of holding governments accountable to and within that system is still a work in progress.)

The best of us have created strategies for survival that are not fueled by xenophobia, so humans may utilize means and modalities that bring peace and prosperity without necessitating the annihilation of the perceived other. Drawing from the most advanced parts of our brains, we seek to understand rather than assume, respect rather than make wrong, honor rather than overpower, and empathize rather than eliminate that which is unfamiliar or unlike us. Compassion gives us the courage to value and appreciate difference instead of fearing or hating it. Through the lens of love, when fear arises, we view it as an invitation to identify our adverse reaction, open to a new opportunity, and evolve in an exchange with the unknown. I believe wholeheartedly that it is only when we move beyond what we know that we truly grow.

---

Today, I invite you to try something unfamiliar or what you consider "foreign." You may go to a new restaurant, order a different type of food, or learn from someone of another culture, race or ethnicity. You might even visit the sacred space of another religion. (If so, be sure to contact them for appropriate hours of visitation.) I am not encouraging cultural tourism but stepping outside your comfort zone to face any fears that may be rooted in prejudice or cultural bias, which you've not previously considered. This is an exercise in mindfulness, self-reflection, cross-cultural sensitivity, and intercultural empathy. As you reflect on this experience, imagine what it might be like to not feel as "at home" in your country or community as you do. If you do not personally know someone for whom this is the case, reflect upon why this might be. What has prevented you from expanding your circle? Extend yourself compassion for what has held you back and let that compassion flow beyond your circle to those you've previously excluded. Practicing cross-cultural compassion has a host of benefits including increased empathy, greater cultural (and self) awareness, enhanced adaptability and cognitive flexibility, better communication, reduced prejudice, the promotion of creativity and inclusivity, and stronger personal and global relationships. I encourage you to explore ways you can understand and appreciate the experience, culture, perspectives, and practices of an individual, racial, ethnic, or religious group with which you cannot relate or are not affiliated; it will benefit you, your community, and our world.

## 29

# YES AND, HELL, NO!

"Our love of lockstep is our greatest curse, the source of all that bedevils us. It is the source of homophobia, xenophobia, racism, sexism, terrorism, bigotry of every variety and hue, because it tells us there is one right way to do things, to look, to behave, to feel, when the only right way is to feel your heart hammering inside you and to listen to what its timpani is saying."

— ANNA QUINDLEN

ONE OF THE MOST LOVING THINGS WE CAN DO IS TRUST ourselves, particularly those of us who have been cautioned against it. One way I learned to trust myself is through somatic awareness or bodily knowing. We are all experts on the voices in our heads, but listening to our bodies is something we must (re)learn and a womanist-feminist exercise that is universally beneficial. Living in a society that prioritizes money, power, whiteness, and maleness compromises our connection with our bodies and our humanity. As a species, we've been tamed into submission, conditioned to conform to societal norms of acceptability and intelligibility. While this process might evoke a sense of security, most of us find it hard to access psychological safety, having been alienated from ourselves, our bodies, and genuine kinship with others in the process.

At 21, I felt "convicted" to tell my pastor, who was also my boss and landlord, that I had major doubts the Bible was inerrant and that I did not believe evangelizing "the lost" was God's will. I also decided to "confess" I had been attracted to women since I was a little Paige. I knew I was taking a chance, but I was conflicted and desperate. His response to me was worse than I anticipated. He told me I was a deceiver and possessed by demons of homosexuality and unbelief. While I would come to understand the lie he (and the evangelical church) led me to believe, at the time I trusted him and his authority and believed "The Enemy" lived inside me. No longer was I attempting to combat the Devil outside, he had evidently infiltrated my body. A similar strategy has been used against BIPOC, women, and queer people across time and around the world to justify Western European colonization under the guise of civilization and Christianization. One way this manifested for women was in the association of the uterus with hysteria in ancient Greece—both words are from the same Greek root (ὑστέρᾱ) and are synonymous. This pseudoscience, and its prevalence up until just over a century ago, represents the misogynistic weaponization of science against women to render them unsound and untrustworthy. The great irony is, of course, the deception and gaslighting by medical doctors (claiming to be experts on women's bodies) proves *them* unsound and untrustworthy. For BIPOC, one of the most dangerous iterations of this strategy has been the vilifying and demonizing of non-Western European cultural traditions to justify the colonization and Christianization of 80% of the world. Ironically, many of the sacred rituals labeled "pagan" and "uncivilized" were later appropriated by Christianity and Western European cultures (e.g., Christmas, Christmas trees, Easter, New Years, Labor Day, Call and Response). These are just two examples of a litany of grievances with the same insidious effect. Once I was told Satan lived inside me, I lost all trust in myself, my intentions, my desires, and any question or aim I pursued. Everything I thought or did was evaluated in view of the (d)evil in me, until I began to connect with my Core Self and the wisdom of my body.

James Baldwin once said, "Take no one's word for anything, including mine, but trust your experience." And to that, I say, "hell, yes!" One of the greatest acts of self-love is found in the reclamation of bodily knowing after having been gaslit. Simply because someone is older, louder, stronger, whiter, more masculine, or has more money, degrees, or ammunition than you does not mean they are trustworthy or more powerful. I wish I had known much earlier than I did that you should not trust the person who says they're right, but tells you you're wrong, the person who asserts they have access to a Truth that you do not, and the one who claims the divine lives outside you and not within you, that an external source must save you, or assures you they love you when they are simultaneously abusing you. Regardless of what you have been told in the past, today, I want you to read the following words and receive them in your heart center: You can trust your body. You can trust your intuition. You can trust your experience. You can trust your knowing. You can trust your wisdom. You can trust yourself. You can trust your "yes," and your "no."

---

Today, notice what it feels like to be in your body. Where is there comfort? Discomfort? Tension? Anxiety? A sense of calm? Once you've gotten in touch with your body, take a moment to reflect on some of the ways you have been led to distrust yourself or made to feel you are untrustworthy. This is not an easy endeavor and may feel uncomfortable, particularly if you've never considered this before. Take your time and trust yourself to know when and if you need to pause, take a break, or move on from this exercise altogether. Once you can access one or two ways in which this has happened, allow space for grief and offer grace because it was not your fault. Next, when you are ready, reframe the statements of self-doubt by affirming your trustworthiness and by naming the ways you can trust yourself; do this even if you do not yet fully believe these things about yourself. Finally, sit in the feeling of trusting yourself and whatever might be arising in your body in this moment. If you find this difficult, just try on trusting yourself and wearing this sort of emotional empowerment around today. When you find yourself slipping back into uncertainty and self-doubt, pull trust and self-assurance back on like a favorite hoodie or a cozy blanket. It is time to trust yourself, your "Hell, yes!" and your "Hell, no!"

# 30

# ZEN

"The real meditation is how you live your life."

— JOHN KABAT-ZINN

IN RECENT YEARS, BUDDHISM, ITS TEACHINGS, AND practices have risen in popularity in the US. Buddhism, which began in India around the 5th century BCE, currently has the most adherents in Asia. While I studied Buddhism in college and was exposed living in Southeast Asia, it was not until I returned to the US, came out, and moved to Northern California, that I felt inclined to deepen my exploration of Eastern philosophy. During my time at Berkeley, I became interested in Buddhism, which led me to take courses at the Institute of World Religions in the Berkely Buddhist Monastery and to begin practicing meditation and, eventually, yoga. I simultaneously became aware of the dangers of cultural appropriation and the ways Americans and Europeans fetishize Asian, Arab, and African cultures. (Courses on decolonizing epistemology and books like

Edward Said's *Orientalism* were as eye-opening and consciousness shifting for me as having lived and/or traveled to all three continents myself.) I came to realize there was a way to honor and appreciate Buddhism, like all non-Western European cultures, which circumvented uncritical appropriation. I consider the concept of Zen to be a helpful lens through which to reflect on the important distinction between appreciation and appropriation as well as self-compassion.

Zen has become a conventional term Americans use to describe being calm or "chill," often doing so without a deeper understanding of the concept, its history or meaning. Researching the etymology of the word leads us to its Chinese roots in the Mahayana Buddhist tradition. *Zen* is a Japanese pronunciation of the Chinese word *ch'an*, which is itself a derivation of the Sanskrit term for "meditation" or total "absorption" (particularly experienced in yoga), *dhyana*. Implementing the word without apprehending or honoring its historical context is a form of appropriation. Cultural appropriation might be understood, then, as taking some aspect of a culture that is not your own and using it for personal interest. The profusion and diffusion of yoga in the US is another excellent example of appropriation since many of us incorporate yoga into our exercise routine with little knowledge of or connection to the history of this ancient practice. (And since about 1 in 3 Americans have at least tried yoga, that's over 100 million of us!) Yoga is much more than a tool for physical fitness, it is a means to access Zen, and appreciating yoga requires doing our due diligence to honor this practice as a culturally rooted modality developed over centuries to bring mind and body into harmony.

Zen emphasizes insight meditation, leading practitioners to the Buddha mind and body; that is, a compassionate and enlightened mind embodied through action in the world. Zen finds its source in lovingkindness and its intention in being fully alive and awake to the nature of reality and the egoless self, whereby one might connect with the wisdom of our interconnectedness. To appreciate the essence and relevance of Zen, then, is to understand it not as a place outside us or a state transcending real life but as a way of life, which leads us toward compassionate connection rather than disinterested disengagement. Meditation, as a vehicle to Zen, is a practice not simply endeavored on a cushion in solitude but expressed in everyday encounters with/in our world. The practice of meditation builds equanimity, clarity, and acceptance, strengthening compassion toward our imperfections, distractions, and triggers, and enabling us to approach others with understanding and empathy. The purpose of meditation is not to feel Zen, but to embody Zen in the world; and what a kinder and more compassionate world this would be if we all appreciated and applied this wisdom.

---

Today, I invite you to meditate for ten minutes. If this is your first time meditating or have tried but feel it is "not your thing" or you just "couldn't turn off your mind," you are not alone—this is a universal experience for beginners and seasoned meditators alike. You may try to meditate by finding some relaxing music without lyrics and setting a timer or, if you have a cell phone, you could use a meditation app. There are a host of great apps (Calm, Insight Timer, Headspace, etc.). Another option is a guided online meditation led by Tara Brach, Pema Chödrön, Thích Nhất Hạnh, Dora Kamau, Tamara Levitt, Kristin Neff, Lama Rod Owens, or Jeff Warren, which you can find by plugging one of their names and "meditation" into your search engine and choosing a video. I have also included some guided meditations for you in the Appendix of this book. I encourage you to give at least one of these a try today.

# EPILOGUE

Love exists in the interstices of tenderness and toughness; it is a purpose, a process, a presence, and the place where we find ourselves simultaneously sensitive and strong. Love opens us to the possibility of hurt, but always with the promise of healing. Love is the paramount paradox, the blessed both/and, which manifests most profoundly through compassion, and true compassion is powered by self-compassion. The protection of our planet and survival of our species is directly proportionate to our capacity to cultivate compassion—to live out of a love for ourselves that of necessity compels us to care for others.

I hope you have found the insights in this companion encouraging and inspiring and that you will continue to practice self-compassion daily. I have compiled a short bibliography of other self-compassion books and workbooks to supplement your practice—my own workbook is forthcoming. If you find after reading *The Self-Compassion Companion* that you are ready and wanting to go deeper in self-compassion as a practice or

## EPILOGUE

would like to work with me as your personal self-compassion coach, please reach out to me at drpaigerawson.com and schedule a free 30-minute consultation or you may find me on Instagram @drpaigerawson. I work with clients individually and with self-compassion cohorts using this resource and my Self-Compassion Curriculum.

I encourage you also to check out the courses offered at the Center for Mindful Self-Compassion (CMSC) and Mindfulness Based Stress Reduction (MBSR) training through mbsrtraining.com or mindfulleader.org.

May you be led to greater compassion and kindness —for yourself and others—and, in so doing, may we, together, transform our world.

## ACKNOWLEDGEMENTS

This book, like my life, would not have been possible without my community. I am because we are.

I would first like to acknowledge Angela and Tehom Center Publishing. Thank you for "getting me" and for loving me enough to nudge me to write the book and guide me through the publication process. I can honestly say I would not have done either if we had not "bopped" back into each other's lives a few years ago. Your intellect, insight, encouragement, and accountability have meant so much to me, especially this year.

I would also like to express deep appreciation for my family of choice: my beloved partner, Ashley, my besties, Keisha and Nana, and my queer cohort. Your endless wisdom, love and support have been a source of great strength for me, one I am thankful I do not have to live without. Each of you has recognized the truth in me and has spoken that truth when I needed to hear it most, relating to me and reminding me who I am and that to which I am called. I am grateful beyond words.

To my Ashley, this paragraph, like my heart, is for

## ACKNOWLEDGEMENTS

you. Your steadfast love and support have helped to ensure this fire keeps burning; it wanes, it grows wild, your love remains. Life with you is all the things and I am exceedingly grateful for every bit of it: the fun and the friction, the dancing and discerning, the growth and the groans, the laughter and the tears, for facing and overcoming fears. You and your healing/self-love journey have encouraged me to continue to rise from the ruin and revel in the wisdom of my experience by sharing it with others; this book is but one of the beautiful byproducts of that process. Your tender care for and belief in me have become a haven and a gentle caress calling me back to self-compassion. Your confidence in and compassion for me repeatedly inspire me to love and believe in myself.

Thank you also to my family of origin. Each of you has contributed in important ways to my life and who I have become. I am grateful to you for your encouragement and motivation in all its fantastic and frustrating forms. Thank you for always making sure I remember from whence I came and that you love me no matter where I go. I love you.

Finally, thank you especially to the great cloud of witnesses around the planet and throughout time on this wild and wide-eyed journey just trying to love and liberate ourselves as we likewise love others on their paths to liberation. Keep doing what you are doing because it is making a difference. I promise.

# APPENDIX

## GUIDED MEDITATIONS

### **Mindful Breathing**

In this attention economy, where our attention is considered a precious commodity, we are inundated with information, advertising, images, and ideas in concert and in competition. As a result, we spend minutes and even hours longer than anticipated searching a topic or scrolling on social media—a pastime that indubitably effects our mental health and wellbeing. It is, therefore, extremely important to exercise our muscle of intention as we direct our attention. Mindful breathing is just one modality we can employ to help strengthen that muscle.

Begin by taking three deep breaths that fill and expand your stomach. With each exhalation, purse your lips and breathe out slowly as if you were cooling off a spoon of hot soup. After you take those breaths, let your breathing continue as per usual and focus on the part of your body where you experience your breath in the most relaxing way. The breath is instrumental in meditation

APPENDIX

because it is always available and requires no special conditions to access. It can also be a mirror for how we are feeling—if we are stressed, it is short, when we are relaxed, it is long. Relatedly, we may energize or relax ourselves through our breathing, shortening it or lengthening it respectively. Play with this at some point today. For now, let the rhythm of your breath soothe you as the air flows in and out of your body. Focus your attention on your breath just under your nostrils, in your chest, or possibly your belly. Drop into the natural rhythm of your body in the breath. Even if it is just for a moment, bring your conscious attention to this involuntary action of the autonomic nervous system. Let yourself be at one with the cycle of inhalation and exhalation as you slowly and intentionally breath. You can calm your mind and body through your breath.

Alternatively, you could focus your attention on a part of your body where you feel any sort of energy, where you find peace or relaxation, or upon your chest or heart center. Send your attention to that area of your body and allow yourself to relax into it. Distracting thoughts will arise, that is just the mind doing what it has been trained to do. There is no need to force those ideas away, acknowledge them politely and, once you have done so, allow them to float off like a cloud in the sky or a leaf on a gently flowing river. (It may help to think of yourself as the sky rather than the clouds or the water and not the leaf.) Your aim here is singular: just breathe and be present right where you are, just as you are. One of the great things about meditation is it gives us access to beginner's mind, where we choose to suspend preconceptions and approach this present moment, time and again, as entirely new and we do so

APPENDIX

with eagerness and wonder. Let whatever arises emerge without judgment, aggression, or fixation. As thoughts, impressions, or sensations surface, it might also help to imagine yourself holding each one gently, like you're holding a balloon by its string. You are attached to the ballon, but it is in your control, and you can release the string at any moment, carefully and on purpose. You may let go whenever you choose, so it does not pull you up and away from the ground or your center of gravity. Through this practice, you are strengthening your connection to your Core Self and your ability to respond to triggers from an equanimous place of clarity, calm, and compassion rather than anxiety, agitation, and aggression.

APPENDIX

## **You Can Do MAGIC**

There are five things I do every morning to ensure I start the day in the healthiest way. Research tells us it takes around two to three months to form a habit. I want to share five habits that make up my morning routine, and I encourage you to try even a few of them for three months (about a quarter of a year). See how they improve your mental health, physical well-being, and your relationships, with yourself and others. I use the acronym MAGIC because I (and my brain) love pneumonic devices, especially acronyms, and because this can help you create magic in your daily life. We cannot control external influences, but we do have power over our responses to them; acting from this conscious place is accessing our MAGIC and here's my 5-step "how to" guide to making magic every day:

**M**editation — The first thing I do every single morning is meditate. I do both guided and unguided meditations for ten to thirty minutes. Meditation is the best way to cultivate mindfulness and to give your brain and body the rest it requires to function at full capacity.

**A**ffirmation — Upon finishing my meditation, I move into affirmations, which include gratitude. This typically takes three to five minutes, but I might allot more time when I have it or if I am struggling. While my affirmations can include "I Am" statements, some mornings it is as simple as me affirming myself and parts of myself I feel need the most love and support at the time. I then express thanks for various people and things in my life. Sometimes this includes a body scan where I move my attention around my body giving love and gratitude for all the parts of me.

**G**entle touch — This can mean offering gentle loving touch to myself or it could involve consensual touch with my partner, a friend, or another loved one. Gentle touch could also extend to companion animals, plants or the earth. Doing this first thing in the morning helps me to continue to offer gentleness to myself and those with whom I interact throughout the day.

**I**ntentional outdoor time — I love the outdoors. I am an athlete, who grew up by the beach and have always loved to hike, camp, and play any sport available to me. I realized early on the health benefits of vitamin D, fresh air, and spending time appreciating Earth's beauty. I recognize and respect that we are not all outdoor enthusiasts, nor do we all have easy access to green spaces and some of us have adverse reactions to nature and extreme climates—much like our ecosystem is having an adverse reaction to our treatment of it. Still, I consider communing with nature a necessity, so I spend at least thirty minutes outside every day. Whether going for a run, walking the dog, watching a sunrise or sunset, or simply stepping out for a deep breath and to feel the sun on my face, intentional time out of doors is mood enhancing, energetically grounding, and reminds us of our intimate relationship to Earth and our environs. I encourage you to find a way to do this at least once a day.

**C**ardiovascular or aerobic exercise — As important as it is to meditate or to take a pause in nature, our minds

APPENDIX

and bodies excel when we incorporate daily exercise. I do not partake in strenuous exercise seven days a week, but it is a part of my schedule at least five. I will not recite the scientific data on the myriad benefits of physical exercise but can attest to the ways it has helped me with emotional regulation, mental function, and the maintenance of a healthy body and strong immune system. I love to run, however, as I age, I've begun to modify my routine to incorporate more cross training. Whether it's running, biking, swimming or another form of aerobic exercise, I try to get my heart rate up to around 60-80% capacity for at least thirty minutes three to five times a week. I encourage you to start slow, set your own goals, and find a running club or group fitness class near you to encourage you and provide accountability.

The percussionist Mickey Hart once said, "Life is about rhythm. We vibrate, our hearts are pumping blood, we are a rhythm machine, that's what we are." Establishing daily routines like these honors our organic rhythms and facilitates new healthy rhythms for us, helping us heal—mind, body, and soul. Try it and you, too, can make MAGIC every single day!

APPENDIX

## Noting

The word mindfulness is derived from the Pali word *sati*, which means "to remember to observe." Mindfulness is a type of meditation as well as a state of nonjudgmental awareness to your present experience. Noting is a mindfulness practice that helps us remember to observe rather than react or overidentify to our experience; it is also one of the most effective ways to deal with fleeting and intrusive thoughts during meditation. Noting is a way to strengthen the muscles of awareness, acceptance, and equanimity. You may do this exercise while stationary or on a walk. Take three deep breaths to center and ground yourself. Make these the deepest and most satisfying breaths you have taken so far today. As you are breathing pay attention to the breath and notice where your mind takes you as you breathe. If it is to your stomach, simply state aloud or to yourself, "stomach," if it is your lungs, say, "lungs," and if it is your nostrils, say, "nostrils." Now, continue to breath normally and as your mind moves around your body or as your eyes look around the room or out in the world, each time you find yourself aware of something, name it. If you feel an itch on your left pinky toe, say, "itch on my left pinky toe." If you see a butterfly or cardinal pass by, say, "butterfly" or "cardinal." If you hear the whir of the fan or an airplane passing overhead, say, "fan" or "airplane." As you allow your mind to move, as it will do, you will be distracted by what you are having for lunch, the conversation that got cut short last night, or those confusing lyrics you really want to Google. This is all okay. Your mind is just doing what the mind does. The important thing is that when this happens, you note it and move right along without judgment or resistance. One of the most common reasons people give up on meditating is because they think that if they think (too much) while they are meditating, they are not meditating; this is not true. Another reason is they get frustrated with their distractibility or inability to concentrate. Sure, we all love to drop into that ideal place during meditation where we aren't distracted by our "monkey minds" and are unmoved by the cares and concerns of everyday life, but it is just not possible to experience that each time we sit. Also, concentration, like awareness, acceptance, and equanimity, is a muscle we build through our commitment to the practice of mindfulness. One of the greatest gifts we give ourselves in meditation is to release ourselves from expectation. Noting is a great way to make light of what our mind does naturally and, instead of expending energy fighting our mind in frustration, we can acknowledge what is happening and enjoy the opportunity to grow in awareness, acceptance, and equanimity.

APPENDIX

## **Zoom In, Zoom Out**

Quite often we overidentify with emotions, so much so that it affects our executive function, making it difficult to see ourselves beyond those emotions much less to regulate them. One way to integrate mindfulness into our daily routine is through a practice I call "Zoom In, Zoom Out" (ZIZO). While this exercise can be done without a journal, like the other meditations included in the Appendix, I encourage you to use a notebook the first time you work with ZIZO.

As we begin, settle into your seat and take a few deep, cleansing breaths. Relax your body as much as possible and imagine your mind's eye is a lens and you are behind the camera, controlling its direction and focus. Call to mind a source of irritation in your life—this could be an overly zealous horn honking tailgater, an inconsiderate customer, an egotistical ex, a narcissistic family member, or a demanding boss. Many practitioners recommend you begin with something mildly disturbing rather than extremely triggering, particularly if this is your first time with such an exercise. I encourage you to choose what or who feels right in this moment. Have you got an instance or an image in your mind? Good. That is your current focal point. Now, with this image in the background, redirect the lens of your mind to focus on the feeling you get in your body when you are in this experience or when you encounter that individual. First, with the lens of your mind's eye, identify *where* you are feeling it, then, use your attention to zoom into *how* you are feeling it. Does it cause a tightness in your chest, do you tense your shoulders or clench your jaw? Maybe it creates pain in your head or discom-

## APPENDIX

fort in your stomach…? As you zoom in, pay close attention to the physical manifestation of these emotions, sit with the intensity of your visceral response, and take in how big it feels when you are this close. As you are paying attention to the emotions evoked and the way they materialize in your body, it is enough just to notice what is coming up for you. Alternatively, you may choose to send yourself some love, as you would offer a loved one or a beloved character in your favorite novel, who is unable to find their way out of a difficult situation.

Once you have zoomed into the intensity of this experience and spent a moment in recognition, I invite you to zoom out. With the lens of your mind's eye, imagine yourself mentally and emotionally stepping back from the situation, as if your camera were gradually pulling away from the scene and capturing the surrounding context in which the interaction took place. What were the influencing factors of which you are aware? What contributed to your specific experience and/or interpretation of events? Is this relationship or experience reminiscent of some other season, place or person in your life? What did you need during that time that you did not get? How might things have gone differently had you had more time, space, or perspective? What can you learn from this situation or relationship about yourself, what you want and need, and what you will no longer tolerate in your life? As you consider these questions, gaze upon yourself in this situation with care, consideration, and compassion. You can see the bigger picture and have the insight to respond from this calmer and more conscious place. Take a moment to acknowl-

APPENDIX

edge and appreciate the way you can be more present with this kind of perspective.

I encourage you to introduce this as a five-to-ten-minute exercise throughout the week and marvel at the way it transforms your approach to everyday inconveniences, strengthening your patience, clarity, and equanimity.

APPENDIX

## Pendulation for Pain Management

I began to experience debilitating migraines in early adolescence, I have since found the source of the pain and learned how to work with it. Many people who suffer with chronic pain utilize medication to manage their discomfort, I believe meditation can also be a beneficial resource in this regard. Pendulation is one of the tools I began using in my early twenties, which is also when I started incorporating meditation into my daily routine. I believe pendulation can be helpful for anyone because, acute or chronic, we all experience pain. Much like "Zoom In, Zoom Out" (ZIZO), pendulation as a practice helps us shift our focus from the source of our suffering to an area of rest and relaxation in our bodies. Instead of walking through the entire verbal sequence, like we do in ZIZO, in this somatic exercise, there are only two to three steps you repeat as little or as often as you like.

In step one, you will access the pain point. Direct all your attention to this area. Acknowledge the pain and breathe into it. In step two, you find a place in or on your body where there is no pain; let's call this the peace or pleasure point. Just as you did with the pain point, direct all your attention to this place and breathe deeply into it. You may stay with this peace point as long as you like. You may find your attention floats back to your pain point naturally. Each time this happens, redirect your conscious awareness to the place of peace where there is no pain on your body. As you feel comfortable, begin playing with your attention, moving it back and forth from the place of pain to that of peace, as if it were a pendulum swinging from one place to another.

As you do so, use the noting technique to notice where there is pain and where there is peace and recognize the difference between. Take time to appreciate your ability to sense the pain and not wholly identify with it.

The third step in this process is optional but can be quite interesting and enjoyable. As you access your peace point, allow your attention to expand this point and move from the original area to other places on/in the body like you would during a body scan. For those unfamiliar with the body scan technique, it is a form of mindfulness meditation wherein we focus our attention on the body and slowly scan it with tender care, noticing every section and sensation without judgment. Combining a body scan with pendulation creates a sort of hybridized pendulation body scan. For example, let's say you are experiencing a headache, but have no pain in your left hand. Once you have accessed, observed, and honored the pain in your head, move your attention to the left hand and feel the peace and even pleasure available there. Appreciate this relief. Now, slowly, move your attention from your hand to your wrist. Is there pain in your wrist? No? Allow your attention to rest in your wrist and enjoy the calm you find there. Once you have spent a moment focusing on the wrist, slowly move your attention to your forearm, from your forearm to your elbow, elbow to upper arm and so on.

Pendulation, as a mindfulness practice, aids us in returning to conscious presence when we are in pain and can help us accept rather than resist that pain. It has been said that suffering is caused by our own resistance to pain. The more we reject pain by expecting life to be other than it is, the more suffering we cause ourselves because we are rejecting the impermanent

APPENDIX

nature of life. While pain can serve as an indicator light, letting us know something needs to be attended to and to heal, the process of healing necessarily entails hurting. Through mindfulness techniques, we can become aware of the source of our pain, consider how to address that pain, and take the important step to acknowledge and accept life as it is, both pleasurable and painful. As we become more awake and aware through mindfulness practices such as these, we come to understand pleasure and pain as sensations rather than permanent states of being. One of the joys of becoming a more conscious human is the ways we grow to see and feel our sensations and emotions as experiences like any other and, rather than identifying with these feelings, we connect with the awareness behind them. From this place, we have the power to choose how we want to respond; may it ever be with compassion.

APPENDIX

## RAIN

On Day 4, I provide a lovingkindness meditation I developed, which I call "The 3 Cs." The 3 Cs (Consciousness, Curiosity, and Compassion) are steps toward responding to ourselves with compassion when we are activated and my personal configuration of years of researching and practicing self-compassion. On Day 19, I provide the three elements of self-compassion Dr. Kristin Neff presents in her book, *Self-Compassion*. In her book, Neff also provides an incredible catalogue of guided self-compassion practices and on her website (www.self-compassion.org), including downloadable MP3s. Another of my favorite self-compassion exercises is Tara Brach's RAIN. This technique involves four steps represented by the acronym RAIN, that is, *Recognize, Allow, Investigate, Nurture*. RAIN is a tool Brach created to aid in the transition from the trance of unworthiness to coming back to full presence—a process she describes as moving us from "being lost in unconscious mental and emotional reactivity to inhabiting our full presence... RAIN creates a clearing in the dense forest" of our minds. According to Brach, RAIN can be applied to any situation in everyday life where we find ourselves overwhelmed enough with mental and emotional static to access the clarity, calm, and compassion of our Core Self. I offer a summary below and encourage you to read *Radical Compassion* for Brach's own explication and application of the method.

Step 1: *Recognize* what is coming up for you as you connect with your own experience (fear, anxiety, guilt,

APPENDIX

anger, sadness, confusion, an acute or chronic trauma response).

Step 2: *Allow* what is happening. If you are afraid, be afraid. If you are anxious, let yourself be anxious. If you are feeling guilty, allow yourself to feel it. According to Brach, we allow by refraining from judgment or trying to fix ourselves. Instead, we choose to breathe and let it be. Even if we do not like what is happening, we let it happen.

Step 3: *Investigate* what feels most difficult. Once we allow, it is possible to go deeper into the truth of what is occurring. In this step, investigate where the tension is located in your body, and why. We feel the physical sensation and ask the scared, anxious, or guilty part of ourselves at least two questions: (1) "What are you believing in this moment?" and (2) "What do you most need right now?"

Step 4: *Nurture* yourself by sending a gentle message to the most tender, aching part of you and giving yourself exactly what you need to hear, know, and feel in that moment. Say what feels comforting or try something like: "I know this is difficult, but I love you and I am here. We've been through the hard before, we made it out then and we will do it again. You will be alright."

I realize this does not work in every single scenario and there are times we cannot access this conscious part of ourselves as well as times when we are genuinely concerned we will not be alright. If you find yourself in a situation where you are having trouble utilizing RAIN,

## APPENDIX

the 3 Cs, or any of these mindfulness tools, please reach out to your therapist, a life coach, a trusted friend or family member, call or text 988 or visit 988lifeline.org. The ability to ask for and receive help is an integral aspect of self-compassion. Reaching out to another when we cannot find the clearing ourselves allows us to overcome isolation and the delusion of detachment, it grants another person the opportunity to show up for us, and it can embolden us to extend compassion to ourselves.

APPENDIX

## Loving Touch

According to therapist Virginia Satir, every human requires four hugs a day for survival, eight for maintenance, and twelve for growth. Many of us do not have that luxury or have not made that a practice because we grew up in homes or environments where we weren't given twelve hugs in a month, much less in one day! Research on attachment has shown the damaging effects of touch deprivation in infancy and early childhood. While we may not be accustomed to giving or receiving physical touch, loving touch can be learned—both in interpersonal relationships and in relation to our self. As the body's largest organ, the skin is remarkably resilient, it is also remarkably sensitive and one easy way to care for and comfort ourselves is by implementing compassionate touch.

Physical touch releases oxytocin and activates the parasympathetic nervous system, calming anxieties, reducing our heart rate, soothing our emotional body, and making us feel safe; research also reveals that oxytocin moderates the mind's bias toward negativity. Offering yourself a loving touch may feel awkward at first and you may even feel self-conscious, but I can assure you the body will respond positively regardless of how your mind represents or registers the gesture. Part of the power of this somatic practice is allowing yourself to engage the body in a compassionate way regardless of how the mind imbues the expression with assessments. I encourage clients to use this exercise whenever they become aware of discomfort or pain in their heart or when they are dealing with a difficult situation. While this mindfulness meditation involves you placing your hand over your heart, other forms of effective soothing touch are placing one or both hands on your abdomen, wrapping your arms around yourself in an embrace, cradling your face in your palms, or rubbing your hands together. When you notice you are feeling stress, anxiety, or hurt:

- Take 2-3 full deep breaths.
- Place your hand over your heart gently and notice the warmth and weight of your hand. (Also try placing both hands on your chest and noticing the difference between the two.)
- Feel your touch. You may rest your hand here or generate a soothing circular motion.
- Feel the natural rise and fall of your chest as you slowly breathe in and out.
- Linger with this feeling for as long as you like, enjoy it.
- As you sit, you may simply connect with your touch or you may also speak tenderly to the part of yourself that is anxious or hurting, saying whatever feels natural or something like, "I see you and understand what you are feeling. I love you and am right here with you in it."
- Return to this practice when and as often as you need.

APPENDIX

## **Express Yourself**

Anne Lamott once said, "Dealing with your rage and grief will give you life. That is both the good news and the bad news: The solution is at hand. Wherever the great dilemma exists is where the great growth is, too." I did not learn this important lesson until somewhere between thirty and forty, and now it is an active part of my self-compassion practice, personally and professionally. The paradox Lamott highlights is integral to living a life of growth rather than stagnation. The very things we so ardently avoid feeling can be catalysts for our healing and transformation. In this exercise, we will be working with anger, but expression as a self-compassion practice can and should be explored with all the core emotions (which include but are not limited to fear, sadness, joy, excitement, and disgust). I will first offer some insights into how we think about anger, ask some important questions for your reflection, and guide you in expressing yourself and your anger in a healthy way.

Anger can be a tricky and sticky emotion. Many of us have been on the receiving end of anger and have the emotional and possibly physical scars to prove it. We may have been disqualified from feeling or expressing anger on account of our race, gender, religion, family system, and in some cases all four. It is also likely that we were led to believe our anger is unacceptable, unrighteous, and/or makes others uncomfortable. Anger, however, is not innately bad or "sinful," it is a core emotion that needs to be expressed like any other. Anger is like a compass or an indicator light that can direct us to identify and express emotions or reveal important things to and about us (like what has been taken from us or what we are afraid to lose). In my opinion, anger is also a pharmakon—an antidote as much as a poison. Anger without love, is most certainly destructive and research indicates that holding our anger inside leads to various health problems including digestive issues, headaches, cardiovascular disease, weakened immune function, and an elevated risk of developing chronic illnesses. The violent expression of anger and anger's suppression are equally as damaging because neither come from a place of love. While anger can be destructive and cause more pain, finding compassionate ways to express our anger can provide an opportunity to heal the pain that lies beneath it.

As you move into this exercise, I invite you first to get as comfortable as possible, relax into your seat, take three deep breaths, and connect with the self-compassion of your Core Self. There are a few stages to expressing yourself and your anger, so give yourself ample time and space to work with this one. In stage one, I'd like for you think of what you were taught about anger as a child. How was anger expressed by the adults and children in the place where you grew up? How did you feel when someone got angry (with you)? Can you recall a time when you felt angry as a child or teenager? What did it feel like in your body? How did you express your anger? Now, I'd like for you to consider something that elicits anger now? It does not have to be the most infuriating thing but choose something that feels similar by degree to the anger you felt in your younger years. Where in your body do you feel anger? What does it feel like? Have you allowed yourself to express this anger before? If so, what happened? Take as long as you need to consider these questions.

APPENDIX

We are now going to shift from reflection to expression. I acknowledge the expression of anger can be a scary endeavor and discomfiting, so as we move into the second phase of this exercise, I encourage you to find a safe place to express your anger. I will provide five different options for you. You may try each of them eventually, but please choose the one that draws you most right now. The following five exercises are healthy means to express your anger and forms of cathartic release.

(1) Ram-page: Take a few pieces of loose-leaf paper—I would encourage you to use unlined paper, so you can write in different sizes and directions all over the paper without the constraint of lines. Ram-paging entails getting all the thoughts, feelings, and everything that angers you out on paper. This does not need to be in narrative form and can include images if that feels beneficial. Reflect upon the situation, who was involved, how you felt, what hurt and angered you, what you needed that you didn't get or what was taken from you, how you feel now, what you need, and anything else that emerges. Feel free to flow freely without holding back. Once you have finished, I encourage you to take the papers and either put them in a safe place or create a ritual to tear or burn them.

(2) Paint the Pain: Find or purchase a set of watercolor paints and some paper. You will use the same prompts as those for ram-paging. Let the emotions flow out of you in color on canvas. Once you have fully released, do whatever feels appropriate with your creation. You may want to share it with someone else, hang it in

APPENDIX

your office, or burn it in a fire pit. Honor what you need.

(3) Work (it) Out: With your anger catalyst in mind, do a strenuous workout. I personally like doing sprints or using a punching bag, but I encourage you to pick the form of exercise that feels right for you and your body. Be aware that if you hold the source of your anger as the engine for your workout, during or after you have completed, you may emote in other ways. There are times I have been moved to tears because moving my body dislodged the pain. If you feel it arising, I encourage you not to hold back. Let it up and out. (Remember this as you decide where you will exercise. It should be a place where you feel safe to be fully yourself.)

(4) Primal Scream: Scream therapy came on the scene in the 1970s and is a legitimate way to re-experience and release repressed emotions. Primal screaming is exactly what it sounds like. Go somewhere private (pillow optional) and allow yourself to scream from your diaphragm and the depth of your pain. I have done this on a mountain top, at the beach, in my room, and in my car, and have even had clients use this one at festivals and live music events. Like every other expression option provided here, your safety and security are paramount, so check in with yourself as you are deciding where, when, and how to access your primal scream. It is difficult enough to try something new, so make sure you feel as comfortable as possible when you do.

(5) Rage Dancing and/or Rage Singing: Find a song or

APPENDIX

songs with music and lyrics that fit your mood. You could even make a playlist, if you need more than a few minutes and want to practice this regularly. Give yourself enough time and room to move, plug in, and get it all out. Remember, when you move your body and vocalize, you are allowing your emotions to do just what they were meant to do: move. So let them move you and move out of you, so you may free them and free yourself from being bound by not expressing them.

Once you finish your chosen modality of expression, take as long as you need to self-soothe, which is the third and final stage of this exercise. I'd encourage you, at the very least, to take a few minutes to check in with yourself and your body and make note of it in your journal. You know what you need better than anyone, but here are some other recommendations for restoration and recalibration: spend a few minutes telling yourself out loud or on paper how proud you are of the courage you have shown in confronting and expressing these difficult emotions, take a nice walk outside and focus on your breathing, listen to some relaxing music or a self-compassion meditation, sit with your pet, take an Epsom salt bath or a shower, get a massage, or share your experience with a trusted friend or confidant. You might also try giving yourself a butterfly hug where you sit in an upright position, close or lower your eyes, slow and deepen your breathing, cross your arms over your chest (fingertips on your collarbones or shoulders), alternate tapping your shoulders or chest, and observe your thoughts, feelings, sensations, images, and any sounds or smells. The cool thing about the butterfly hug is that it activates both hemispheres of the brain simultaneously

APPENDIX

leading to a more harmonious state. This bilateral stimulation (BLS) calms the nervous system, so it's a great practice to use when you're stressed, anxious, or overwhelmed by an emotion, since it helps us self-regulate by reducing the amygdala's activity and secreting serotonin and dopamine as well as aiding in the reprocessing of traumatic memories. If you feel that after this experience, you'd like to go even deeper in your own self-exploration and healing, I encourage you to find a local EMDR (Eye Movement Desensitization and Reprocessing) therapist (https://www.emdria.org/find-an-emdr-therapist/) or contact me at drpaigerawson@gmail.com.

# BIBLIOGRAPHY

## SELF-COMPASSION RESOURCES

Becker, Michelle. *Compassion for Couples: Building the Skill of Loving Connection*. New York: Guilford Press, 2023.

Beltzner, Eileen. *How to Tame the Tumbles: The Mindful and Compassionate Way*. Ontario: Mosaic Press, 2019.

Bertin, Mark, and Karen Bluth. *Mindfulness and Self-Compassion for Teen ADHD: Build Executive Functioning Skills, Increase Motivation, and Improve Self-Confidence*. The Instant Help Solutions Series, 2021.

Blackwell, Kelsey, and Christena Cleveland. *Decolonizing the Body: Healing, Body-Centered Practices for Women of Color to Reclaim Confidence, Dignity, and Self-Worth*. Oakland: New Harbinger, 2023.

Bluth, Karen. *The Self-Compassion Workbook for Teens: Mindfulness and Compassion Skills to Overcome Self-Criticism and Embrace Who You Are*. Oakland: New Harbinger, 2017.

Bluth, Karen. *The Self-Compassionate Teen: Mindfulness and Compassion Skills to Conquer Your Critical Inner Voice*. The Instant Help Solutions Series, 2020.

Brach, Tara. *Radical Acceptance: Embracing Your Life with the Heart of a Buddha*. New York: Bantam, 2003.

Brach, Tara. *Radical Compassion: Learning to Love Yourself and Your World with the Practice of Rain*. New York: Penguin, 2020.

Brown, Brene. *The Gifts of Imperfection*. Center City, MN: Hazelden, 2010.

Chödrön, Pema. Start Where You Are: A Guide to Compassionate Living. Boulder: Shambala, 2018.

Dabbs, Kim. *You Belong Here: The Power of Being Seen, Heard, and Valued on Your Own Terms*. Oakland: Barret-Koehler, 2024.

Desmond, Tim. *Self-Compassion in Psychotherapy: Mindfulness-Based Practices for Healing and Transformation*. Norton, 2015.

Garcia, Gabi. *Listening with My Heart: A story of kindness and self-compassion*. Gabi Garcia Books, 2017.

Germer, Christopher K. *The Mindful Path to Self-Compassion: Freeing Yourself from Destructive Thoughts and Emotions*. New York: Guilford Press, 2009.

Germer, Christopher K., and Kristin D. Neff. *Teaching the Mindful Self-

*Compassion Program: A guide for professionals.* New York: Guilford Press, 2019.

Gilbert, Paul. *The Compassionate Mind.* London: Constable, 2009.

Harris, Farah. *The Color of Emotional Intelligence: Elevating Our Self and Social Awareness to Address Inequities.* Working Well Daily, 2023.

Hendel, Hillary Jacobs. *It's Not Always Depression: Working the Change Triangle to Listen to the Body, Discover Core Emotions, and Connect to Your Authentic Self.* New York: Penguin Random House, 2018.

Hersey, Tricia. *Rest is Resistance: A Manifesto.* New York: Little Brown Spark, 2022.

Hickman, Steven. *Self-Compassion for Dummies.* Hoboken, NJ: John Wiley, 2021.

Hobbs, Lorraine M., and Amy C. Balentine. *The Self-Compassion Workbook for Kids: Fun Mindfulness Activities to Build Emotional Strength and Make Kindness Your Superpower.* Instant Help Solution Series, 2023.

Hobbs, Lorraine M., and Nina Tamura. *Teaching Self-Compassion to Teens.* Guilford Publications, 2022.

Izadi, Shahroo. *The Kindness Method: Change Your Habits for Good Using Self-Compassion and Understanding.* New York: St. Martin's, 2019

Johnson, Rachel. *Self-Love Workbook for Black Women. Empowering Exercises to Build Self-Compassion and Nurture Your True Self.* Oakland: Callisto, 2022.

Magee, Rhonda. *The Inner Work of Racial Justice: Healing Ourselves and Transforming Our Communities Through Mindfulness.* New York: TarcherPerigee, 2019.

Manning, Roxy, and Sarah Peyton. *The Anti-Racist Heart: A Self-Compassion and Activism Handbook.* Oakland: Berrett-Koehler, 2023.

Marlowe, Sara. *My New Best Friend.* Summerville, MA: Wisdom Publications, 2016.

Neff, Kristin D., and Christopher K. Germer. *The Mindful Self-Compassion Workbook: A Proven Way to Accept Yourself, Find Inner Strength, and Thrive.* New York: Guilford Press, 2018.

Neff, Kristin D. *Fierce Self-Compassion: How Women Can Harness Kindness to Speak Up, Claim Their Power, and Thrive.* New York: Harper Wave, 2021.

Neff, Kristin D. *Self-Compassion: The Proven Power of Being Kind to Yourself.* New York: William Morrow, 2021.

O'Leary, Wendy. *It's OK: Being Kind to Yourself When Things Feel Hard.* Bala Kids, 2023.

Pollak, Susan M. *Self-Compassion for Parents: Nurture Your Child by Caring for Yourself.* New York: Guilford Press, 2019.

# BIBLIOGRAPHY

Quinlan, Kimberly. *The Self-Compassion Workbook for OCD: Lean into Your Fear, Manage Difficult Emotions, and Focus on Recovery.* Oakland: New Harbinger, 2021.

Russ, Terri L. *Cultivating Compassion, Creating Self: Meditations on Transforming Fear into Creativity.* St. Petersburg, FL: Tehom, 2024.

Salzberg, Sharon. *Lovingkindness: The Revolutionary Art of Happiness.* Boulder: Shambala, 1995.

Schwartz, Richard. *No Bad Parts: Healing Trauma and Restoring Wholeness with the Internal Family Systems Model.* Boulder: Sounds True, 2021.

Shapiro, Shauna. *Good Morning, I Love You: Mindfulness and Self-Compassion Practices to Rewire Your Brain for Calm, Clarity, and Joy.* Boulder: Sounds True, 2020.

Silberstein-Tirch, Laura. *How to Be Nice to Yourself: The Everyday Guide to Self-Compassion.* San Antonio, TX: Althea Press, 2019.

Taylor, Sonya Renee. *The Body is Not an Apology: The Power of Self-Love.* Oakland: Berret-Koehler, 2018.

Tawwab, Nedra Glover. *Set Boundaries, Find Peace: A Guide to Reclaiming Yourself.* New York: Penguin Random House, 2021

Van der Kolk, Bessel A. *The Body Keeps the Score: Brain, Mind and Body in the Healing of Trauma.* New York: Penguin Books, 2014.

Quraishi, Zahabiya. *You are Love: Nurturing Self-Love and Self-Esteem in Muslim Girls.* 2023.

# NATIONAL HELPLINE NUMBERS

Substance Abuse and Mental Health Services Administration (SAMHSA) National Helpline
1-800-662-HELP (4357)
SAMHSA operates 24/7 and provides information and referrals if you or a loved one are facing mental health and/or substance use issues. The confidential service does not provide counseling, but can direct you to helpful resources, including treatment facilities and support groups in your area.

National Suicide Prevention Lifeline
Call 988
NSPL is a national toll-free number that operates 24/7 and connects to local crisis centers where a trained worker will provide confidential support to people experiencing suicidal thoughts or emotional distress.

Crisis Text Line
Text 741741
Many people, especially teenagers and young people,

NATIONAL HELPLINE NUMBERS

are growing up more comfortable texting. The Crisis Text Line serves anyone in the United States with this confidential and free 24/7 text line, connecting you with a trained crisis counselor.

National Domestic Violence Hotline
1-800-799-SAFE (7233) or text "LOVEIS" to 22522
Operates 24/7 and provides confidential assistance to anyone experiencing domestic violence or questioning if they are in an abusive relationship. Online chat with trained advocates is available through the website (https://www.thehotline.org/).

National Eating Disorders Association (NEDA) Helpline
1-800-931-2237 or Text "HOME" to 741-741
The NEDA Helpline is available Monday through Friday and offers phone, chat, and text support for yourself or a loved one coping with an eating disorder.

LGBT National Hotline
1-888-843-4564
The LGBT National Hotline operates Monday through Saturday and provides one-to-one peer support in a confidential, safe space for anyone to discuss issues with coming out, gender or sexual identity, relationship concerns, bullying, self-harm, and more.

The Trevor Project
1-866-488-7386 or Text "START" to 678678
The Trevor Project is a national organization providing 24/7 crisis intervention to LGBTQ youth with phone, chat, and text options.

## NATIONAL HELPLINE NUMBERS

National Runaway Safeline
1-800-RUNAWAY (1-800-786-2929)
The National Runaway Safeline is a 24/7 crisis hotline, online service, and judgment-free safe space for runaways and unhoused young people.

Rape Abuse and Incest National Network (RAINN)
1-800-656-HOPE (4673)
The 24/7 RAINN Helpline has phone and online chat options (https://rainn.org/). RAINN provides access to support from trained staff, who can direct you to local health facilities with experience caring for survivors of sexual assault, as well as resources for healing, recovery, long-term support, and more.

Childhelp National Child Abuse Hotline
1-800-4-A-Child or 1-800-422-4453
Dedicated to preventing child abuse, Childhelp operates 24/7, and is staffed by professional crisis counselors and translators who provide help and emergency/social service referrals in over 170 languages. Their website (https://www.childhelphotline.org/) provides online chat with a trained professional.

SAMHSA Disaster Distress Helpline
1-800-985-5990 or Text "TalkWithUs" to 66746
SAMHSA's Disaster Distress Helpline is available 24/7 to anyone in the US and its territories and provides immediate crisis counseling if you are experiencing stress, anxiety, and other symptoms resulting from human-made or natural disasters (including pandemics).

NATIONAL HELPLINE NUMBERS

National Alliance on Mental Illness (NAMI) HelpLine
1-800-950-NAMI (6264)
The NAMI Helpline is a nationwide peer-support service, and *not* a crisis line, that provides information, resource referrals, and community support if you or someone you know are living with a mental health condition.

www.ingramcontent.com/pod-product-compliance
Lightning Source LLC
Chambersburg PA
CBHW050256010526
44107CB00033B/1393/J